How to
Attract
the
Wombat

How to
Attract
the
Wombat

WILL CUPPY

ILLUSTRATIONS BY
ED NOFZIGER

SUTTON PUBLISHING

For Marione

This book was first published in 2001 by David R. Godine

This edition first published in 2007 by
Sutton Publishing Limited · Phoenix Mill · Thrupp · Stroud
Gloucestershire · GL5 2BU

Copyright © 2001 by Phyllis Feldkamp

For permission to use all the short animal pieces and two others
which appear here in longer versions the author thanks the *Saturday
Evening Post*. "Swan-upping, Indeed!" was first printed in *The New
Yorker*. Certain other articles of particular interest to Wombat
enthusiasts were written especially for this book.

British Library Cataloguing in Publication Data
A catalogue record for this book is available from the British Library

ISBN 978-0-7509-4610-0

Printed and bound in England.

CONTENTS

❖ ❖ ❖

How to Attract the Wombat

ARE WOMBATS PEOPLE?

It would appear, from the record, that I have written my third animal book. *How to Tell Your Friends from the Apes* was published in 1931, *How to Become Extinct* in 1941. Perhaps I should have waited until 1951 before offering *How to Attract the Wombat*, just to make the dates come out even, but I felt I had things to say about the Wombat which needed to be said at this time.

This volume completes, at least in part, a project conceived some twenty years ago, when I first thought of writing a series of "How" books which should deal with various aspects of the animal world that particularly interested me, and at the same time rescue me from a rather sordid economic situation, leaving me free for certain other activities I had in mind, such as batting around and having a little fun in my old age. Well, life is like that.

As for this third attempt, the public in general may of

course decide that I've already done enough for the animals. This nasty thought occurred to me the other day on the street when an old friend came along and inquired, "Are you still writing those little animals?" I was particularly struck, and not favorably, by this question because I have written about some of the largest animals in existence. I do think the elephant should be big enough for anybody, and how about the Sulphur-bottom Whale, the largest animal in the seven seas, sometimes reaching a length of a hundred feet and weighing up to a hundred and fifty tons? What more does he expect?

I'm only fooling, for I know well enough that the fellow meant to ask, "Are you still writing those little pieces about animals?" I should have replied, as I usually do: "Yes, I am still writing little pieces about animals. I am a person who writes little pieces about animals. I am in that business. That is what I do. See?" I didn't care to make the effort again. I merely nodded noncommittally and walked away, with the curt remark, "Nice seeing you again."

I knew so well what the fellow was leading up to, and there are times when I can't take it. In another ten seconds, or make it five, he would have asked, "Why don't you write about *people*, Will?" They always do. They have, through the years. They will, as long as I am spared. It is a cross I must bear.

To give you an idea, the first friend I met on the street after writing that book on Apes fought her way through the crowd as soon as she saw me and shouted from afar, "Why don't you write about *people*, Will?" This surprised me the more since I had used that very lady as the model for my article on the Chimp in that volume. I was afraid she would sue, but, as seems to be routine with my works, nothing happened. In *How to Attract the Wombat* she appears again as the main character in my chapter on the Goose, but she will never know it. She thinks I am not interested in people.

Was it for this, I often ask myself, that I have risked my scientific reputation time after time by an outrageously anthropomorphic treatment of the animals, that I have played fast and loose with the accepted distinctions between instinct and intelligence to the point of endangering some of the fundamental principles of Darwin himself, until I probably couldn't get the most menial job in a respectable Zoo?

Why do you suppose I did that unless it was to get in all those dirty cracks about the human race, a form of life I suppose I am a little too much inclined to look down upon. By the way, I must try to get over that or my views will become distorted in time. Not interested in people, indeed!

But they mean well, bless them. They want me to get ahead. They bring me examples of authors, from dim antiquity to this morning's papers, who have risen by easy stages or even jumped instantaneously to the top of their profession by writing about people. Some of these friends have done well in their chosen fields of endeavor. A few of them have what it takes, and God knows they hang on to it. Maybe I should listen to their advice.

Maybe, in response to what I can only regard as public demand, I should write a book about people plainly labeled and certified as such, so that there could be no possible mistake. Then they could ask me, "Why don't you write about *animals*, Will?" It would be a change.

And now a word on the Wombat. What is it? Animal, vegetable, or mineral? Give up? I feel justified in asking these forthright questions because the ignorance that prevails on the subject is simply frightening. "I know nothing about the Wombat except that it lays eggs and barks," said a lady on whom I was counting for useful information. And when I asked a man whom I had always supposed to be fairly civilized if he had ever heard of the Wombat, he replied, "Sure, he played third base on the Yankees in '35." Ninety-nine others merely said No. Really, I sometimes wonder what *is* the use.

For reasons of my own, I am not telling at this point exactly what a Wombat is or is not. I assure you, though, that the Wombat exists. In the Wombat we are confronted by a fact, not a theory. That is all I care to divulge at the moment as I prefer, in the interest of suspense, to keep the reader on tenterhooks until he comes to the article entitled "The Wombat" under the larger heading, "Problem Mammals."

There, I've gone and dropped a hint that gives part of the secret away. So the Wombat is a mammal! If I know my public, however, no great harm has been done, for I find the widest divergence of opinion on what is a mammal. Five of my acquaintances, when asked to define a mammal, replied, "Well, the Cow is a mammal." That is correct. Four others said, "Well, the Whale is a mammal." Right again, but two of these had been going through life with the erroneous impression, drawn from that fragment of truth, that mammal is only a more dignified name for fish. That is what comes of teaching innocent children what a Whale is. Something should be done about this.

I had no better luck with the young woman, a graduate of one of our foremost institutions of learning, whom I asked to define a marsupial, a special kind of mammal that comes into the plot later on. After she had flunked on the mammals in general by guessing that a mammal is any animal that is quite large (and I must confess there is a sort of fundamental rightness in that view that I hesitate to disturb), she stated that a marsupial was something from the polar regions, and stuck to it. She could give no rational explanation, during a rather painful cross-questioning, of how such an association had occurred to her, and I wound up by feeling glad that she had heard of the polar regions at least — on the radio, doubtless. Naturally, I apologized for what must have seemed to her a display of heartless brutality. I can't bear to see a woman cry.

As for the title of this book, of course it is stolen from, or let us say inspired by, that invaluable little volume I am always running across, *How to Attract the Birds*, by Robert S. Lemmon. Heaven forbid that I should ever attract a bird, or birds, but you can see how that title solved my problem when I was fumbling around for one of my own. If you knew my private opinion of birds, you would understand why I consider my version an improvement, with all respect to Mr. Lemmon. The whole subject of ornithology stirs me so profoundly that I mustn't go into it here. There isn't time. I will only say that the more I see of birds, the better I like Wombats.

There are moments, I may add, when my title, *How to Attract the Wombat*, does not entirely satisfy me. There's something a little cold, a little remote, about using a generic term like "the Wombat" when it's a question of attracting him. Nobody writes a book called *How to Attract the Man*, or *How to Attract the Woman*, so I took to favoring *How to Attract a Wombat* as more in tune with what really goes on, more urgent, more immediate, more business-like. Then I would wake up in the night thinking of people who might

want to attract a lot of Wombats. Would they buy a book enabling them to attract one Wombat, or must I change the wording to *How to Attract Wombats*, in the plural? All those I consulted on these variations at the last moment said yes, they guessed it was all right if I liked it, and indicated that the subject, so far as they were concerned, was closed.

I suppose there are people who do not wish to attract even one Wombat, let alone a number of them. Most of these are simply indifferent. They do not care, one way or the other. Has it never occurred to them that they may be missing something, and that it might be Wombats? I am afraid their present attitude, if they persist in it, may occasion our sales manager more than one *mauvais quart d'heure* before he is through with it.

On the other hand, considering what we have learned of our fellow creatures in recent years, there are undoubtedly those who do wish to attract a Wombat or Wombats, just why is not for me to inquire. For them this book could be a treasure worth many times the price of admission. I might even say it would fill a long-felt want.

Finally a word to the more respectable of my readers, some of whom may be shocked by certain sensational passages I slipped into the text during final revision, just in case. God bless them all. I would not willingly bring a blush to their cheeks or upset them in any way, manner, shape or form whatever. Still and all, I realize that a book which hopes to receive even passing attention today must be pretty snappy in regard to you-know-what. In preparing my material for the printer, therefore, I have kept constantly in mind our large and growing body of sex maniacs. They read books too.

Mammals
for Beginners

❖   ❖   ❖

THE MOUSE

You may not care much for Mice but they exist just the same. In fact, there are more Mice in the world than any other mammal.[1] Wherever you are, there is a Mouse not far away. He may be closer than you think. Mice of all kinds are extremely prolific. Mother Mice have babies all the year round, from four to thirteen at a time. They don't know when to stop.[2] Young Mice grow up very quickly. They leave the nest and start something when they are only a few weeks old, and it is always the same old story. So I guess Mice will go on forever. The House Mouse is found in all civilized places and in some others I might mention. Mouseologists say House Mice are not native American Mice as they were introduced from abroad, but who wasn't? House Mice settled in Jamestown in 1607 and more came on the Mayflower in 1620. Unless he arrived on the last boat, any Mouse chosen at random has more ancestors born in this country than any Mouseologist of my acquaintance, so why be stuffy about it? The Field Mouse and the White-footed Mouse

1 We have plenty of Rats, too.
2 Aristotle states that Mice conceive by licking salt. Some of them do, maybe.

11

were here even before 1492 and you don't hear them heckling us on the subject, either. House Mice are loyal little creatures. They will stay with you to the last crumb. They sample everything in the pantry and you can hardly blame them.[3] Mice believe chocolate layer cakes grow wild for the general good. They think life is like that. It should be. Once in a while a Mouse will sneak into the living room to watch you at your strange antics, and you may decide to let him stick around, he looks so friendly and intelligent.[4] You think it will be great fun to have a Mouse of your own. Besides, it will give the Mouse a real home and a sense of security.[5] A Mouse will live with anybody. Some evening you may notice that he isn't the same Mouse and that another one seems to be streaking across the floor just for the hell of it. A check-up will probably reveal that you now have fourteen Mice, most of them expecting — which was not your original idea at all. Moral: It is practically impossible to have one Mouse.

3 In Sanskrit the Mouse was called Mush, from a verb meaning "to steal." Oh, yes? And how did they come to have such a verb?
4 Most House Mice trained in a laboratory can find their way out of a trick box or maze if you give them enough trials. I could do that myself.
5 Tossing bits of cheese to a Mouse is a mistaken kindness. Cheese is bad for Mice.

THE SQUIRREL

The Squirrel is out for a good time. He rushes through the treetops, plays tag with the other Squirrels, eats all the nuts he can hold, and generally behaves as though the world was made for that sort of thing. He is so glad to be alive that nobody has any respect for his mental powers. If you told a Squirrel that life is real and life is earnest, he would dash up the nearest tree, get out on a limb, and offer you a few choice remarks meaning that you are plumb crazy.[1] Squirrels are natural comics and nobody knows it better than squirrels. Anything for a laugh.[2] They will sit up on their haunches and gnaw at a walnut, turn flip-flops, leap from branch to branch and go through their whole bag of tricks for an audience of one, but they would rather have more. They realize this is part of their job as squirrels. They are fine at it, too, and all it gets them is a reputation for shallowness and irresponsibility.

1 Squirrels make little or no use of what we call thinking. They seem to be doing all right.
2 Squirrels of all kinds make entertaining pets. Some species do not bite much.

Does that strike you as fair? Ask an Owl his opinion of the Squirrel and he will whoo-whoo in a most superior tone of voice. Look who's talking![3] Squirrels have been criticized for hiding nuts in various places for future use and then forgetting the places. Well, Squirrels do not bother with minor details like that. They have other things on their mind, such as hiding more nuts where they can't find them.[4] The Squirrel is very inquisitive about young people who go into the woods to pick wild flowers. To judge by his scolding, he strongly disapproves of this pastime, so he follows them around in the hope of seeing more. Squirrels are very moral mammals. A couple will live together year after year with no other interests, and they seem to enjoy it.[5] During the winter they live in their nest in a hollow tree, often remaining indoors for several days at a stretch. I wonder how they manage to kill the time, without any reading to do. And then again, they will feel an urge for fresh air. If you're out some bright, snappy morning, you're likely to see Mr. Squirrel chasing his mate hither and yon over the landscape, snow or no snow. I am often asked why there are so many Squirrels. I don't know.

3 What the Squirrel says about the Owl is extremely amusing. We won't go into it here.
4 The Red Squirrel or Chickaree can hardly exist without pine cones. The Gray or Central Park Squirrel will settle for peanuts.
5 I always said we could learn something from Squirrels.

THE RABBIT

The Rabbit, or Bunny, is a perfect darling. He sits on the lawn, twitching his nose and wiggling his ears and looking so innocent that you feel all soft and protective. That is the way the rabbit wants you to feel. He has just finished the last of your string beans and as soon as you turn your back he is going to eat your pet petunia.[1] He knows you will be pretty sore but you will forgive him because you are a weak character. You always give him a break, so he figures you are slightly half-witted. Rabbits have no important thoughts. Their brains are quite smooth and unwrinkled, from lack of mental exercise. They do not even try. Our brains are full of contortions and convolutions, showing that we have made an effort at least. Be that as it may, Rabbits are able to multiply at the age of four months without any previous training. It must come natural. Rabbits are seldom the homebody type. Here and there a Rabbit will have the same mate for awhile, but they are not

1 Rabbits chew on the bias simply to be cute.

fanatics on the subject. They have excellent eyesight and what they miss is hardly worth seeing.[2] Rabbits need a good talking to, especially the males.[3] Hares and Rabbits are said to be mad in March, when they race around in the moonlight, kicking up their heels. They feel good in March. What's so peculiar about that? Some authorities insist that the Cottontail Rabbit is really a Hare. They are wasting their breath, for we all know a Rabbit when we see one. Officially, the Jack Rabbit is also a Hare and the Belgian Hare is a Rabbit. The English or Jugged Hare is out of luck.[4] Many persons have lived useful and happy lives without learning all the slight technical differences between the Rabbit and the Hare, so why worry?[5] Rabbits and Hares are only rodents, anyhow. We are far superior to the rodents in all sorts of ways. For example — well, I'm sure I could think of a lot of ways if you'd give me a little more time.

2 Rabbits do not sleep with their eyes open and let's not argue.
3 They would reply that you're only young once. It's a point.
4 The ancients said that Hares run faster uphill than down. Times have changed.
5 You've got along so far, haven't you?

THE ARMADILLO

How much do you really know about the Armadillo? I thought
so. The Armadillo is a mammal, which seems to surprise some
people. Perhaps I should have studied these people instead of
the Armadillo. It would be a life work, however, and I haven't
time for it now. The Armadillo wears a coat of armor consisting of bony shields fore and aft, and tough, flexible bands
across the middle of his back. This protects him against possible attack from above. While the Armadillo is thinking how
safe he is on top, some other mammal flips him upside down
and has a nice meal of raw Armadillo. Let that be a lesson.[1]
The Three-banded Armadillo of South America is the only
kind that rolls himself into a complete ball, with his head, legs
and tail inside somewhere. The others can't do this and you
mustn't expect it. When a Monkey jumps on him in the forest,
the ball starts rolling around every which way and the joke is
on the Monkey.[2] The Nine-banded Armadillo of Texas and a

1 As they trot around in the grass, rooting for insects and such, Armadillos
remind some observers of young Pigs. Oddly enough, young Pigs never
remind them of Armadillos.
2 Three-banded Armadillos have muscles which prevent injury to their
internal organs while temporarily squeezed or displaced in the ball phase.
They think of everything.

17

few other places is the only one we have in the United States.[3] The females always give birth to quadruplets, all of the same sex. They can't tell the children apart, and why should they? The bony shell of the Nine-banded Armadillo is about fifteen inches long and is made into ornamental baskets for the tourist trade. In Armadillo society all the individuals are born free and equal. Every young Armadillo starts life with exactly the same chance to become a basket. Nine-banded Armadillos are said to make affectionate pets. You can lead them about on a leash, but you're likely to stop the traffic. People rush from all directions and ask you what you are selling.[4] The Thirteen-banded Armadillo considers himself a genius, as most Armadillos cannot count above nine. The Pichiciago or Fairy Armadillo of Argentina is only five inches long, with a pink shell and silky white sideburns. Fairy Armadillos are somewhat rare, but they can always be found if you know the right places. They come out at dusk. The Glyptodon, an ancient relative of the Armadillo, reached a length of ten or twelve feet and his armor was an inch thick. He hung around for millions of years, but he never got anywhere and finally became extinct. Nobody wanted any baskets of that size.

3 Nine-banded Armadillos are spreading eastward and northward. Persons who transport Armadillos across rivers are known as Armadillo carriers.
4 The natives of Yucatan believe the Black-headed Vulture in old age turns into an Armadillo. I doubt it.

THE PORCUPINE

Nobody loves the Porcupine and I'm afraid it is all his own fault. His back and tail are covered with sharp spines, or quills, the purpose of which I will tell you in a moment.[1] When he is left entirely alone the Porcupine is mild and inoffensive, attending strictly to his own affairs and never going out of his way to attack his neighbors. If one of them comes too close, however, he raises his quills, shoves himself backward and lashes his tail right and left with most unpleasant results.[2] The Porcupine has been known to inflict fatal injuries upon Pumas and Lynxes who were only looking for a bit of lunch. As the Porcupine makes fine eating, the other animals do not like his attitude.[3] Professor Halstead recently achieved some success in teaching a Porcupine to relax. His

1 The quills of the Old World Porcupine may be more than a foot in length. Those of the New World Porcupine are much shorter. They feel about the same.

2 The Brazilian Tree Porcupine curls his long prehensile tail around branches in a counter-clockwise direction. Spider Monkeys do it clockwise.

3 Porcupines do not shoot their quills from any distance, great or small. If one of my readers has been shot by a Porcupine, that's different.

subject had learned to keep his quills down when approached and seemed on the road to further improvement, then along came a big Grizzly Bear and spoiled the experiment. Professor Halstead is now checking his data to see where he went wrong. A Porcupine caught in infancy can be trained to follow his owner around like a Dog. This is nice for people who wish to be followed by Porcupines.[4] In my opinion, relations between Porcupines and people will never be ideal because it would be impossible to give every Porcupine a course in good manners. They become furious if you merely poke them with a stick or try to pull out a few quills for souvenirs. The quills are covered with barbs and are extremely difficult to remove from one's physique. Pet Porcupines like to climb into your lap for an afternoon snooze, a habit that may strike you as awfully sweet and cozy. Personally, I'd rather have my health. You will be happier in the long run if you avoid the Porcupine and all his works. Then the problem of how to extract the quills will not be likely to arise. I always say there are so many things to do in this world, why get involved with Porcupines? Porcupines do not have much fun, but some. Two Porcupines in a hollow tree are too many, as they are always rolling over suddenly and wounding anyone near them. The average Porcupine prefers to live alone and no wonder. He feels that another Porcupine wouldn't be much to come home to.

4 I once knew a man who had a pet Porcupine. Or, rather, I saw him once and I heard a good deal about him. I never even met him.

ADVANCED
MAMMALS

❖ ❖ ❖

THE TAPIR

Tapirs are animals used in geography books. Geography could be taught without Tapirs but it would not be the same. Geography with Tapirs gives children the right start in life. If they go wrong later on, it is not the fault of the Tapir. The Tapir's most prominent feature is his short flexible trunk, or proboscis, made of his nose and upper lip. It is not much good and it spoils his appearance. As Tapirs are built close to the ground they have no need of trunks, but it is too late to do anything about it now. The Tapir has a rudimentary tail, so he is a sight both coming and going. He resembles a Hog with proboscis trouble, but don't tell that to a Tapir. He thinks he looks like a Horse because he has a thin, skimpy mane on his neck. He trots and gallops and fools nobody.[1] The South American Tapir is brownish and so are Baird's Tapir and Dow's Tapir of Central America.[2] The Malayan or Two-toned Tapir is black fore and aft with a whitish middle because he believes in dis-

1 The Tapir is distantly related to the Horse in a collateral sort of way. He is also a cousin of the Rhinoceros, a fact he would rather forget.
2 Dr. Baird and Captain Dow always maintained that their Tapirs were a little different from all other Tapirs. Maybe so.

ruptive coloration. When lying down he looks exactly like a big gray rock. That is, he thinks he does. All baby Tapirs have light longitudinal stripes and spots which render them invisible to some people in the sun-flecked forest. Their mother sees them and I see them but these people go tripping over them all the time. I may be peculiar. I can see striped objects as well as plain ones, if not better. Baby Tapirs are simply wonderful but they soon get over that. The male Tapir never visits his family. He never knows the comforts of a home full of romping young Tapirs and the joys of a life-long companionship with a female Tapir. That sort of thing is exactly what he doesn't want and he arranges his life so that he doesn't get it. No, he is not lonely.[3] All the Tapir asks is a quiet life in the woods and streams. He avoids the Anaconda, the Jaguar, and Man.[4] The Tapir is an odd-toed ungulate, with only three toes on his hind feet. From some points of view it is better to have an even number of toes, for odd-toed ungulates are more likely to become extinct.[5] Besides, Tapirs refuse to adapt themselves to modern conditions. They hate modern conditions even more than I do, so I'm afraid they are on their way out. Now, don't get all upset about it. That won't help matters in the least.

3 Buffon called the Tapir a gloomy and melancholy animal. Only sometimes.
4 Tapirs feel fairly safe in the Zoo, where they are protected by iron bars.
5 The Hog is an even-toed ungulate. There will always be Hogs.

THE LLAMA

Llamas live in South America, where they have been domesticated for centuries. They were employed by the Incas of Peru to carry things up and down the Andes and they have been doing it ever since.[1] It seems to be their one aim in life. Llamas got the double "l" in their name from the Spaniards, who conquered the Incas in 1533.[2] The Spaniards had this double "l" knocking around in their alphabet, so they hung it on the poor Llama. They pronounce it Lee-ah-ma because that is correct in Spanish.[3] Llamas like to be in high mountainous regions where the rarefied air would be bad for most animals. As Llamas have never heard of oxygen they do not miss it. Llamas are members of the Camel group, but they went their own way long ago and lost the family resemblance. This was a mistake for now they look like Llamas.[4] I can't put my finger on it right now, but something is wrong with them somewhere. It may be

1 You remember Atahuallpa, don't you? Why not?
2 Pizarro. Does that ring a bell?
3 The English pronounce it Lay-ma because they are English.
4 Some say the Llama looks like a Camel without a hump. It is impossible to look like a Camel without a hump.

the neck. The Llama is good in arithmetic and will carry only a hundred pounds on his back. If you load him with more than that, he will lie down in the middle of the road and refuse to budge until the weight is checked and adjusted. He will get up when he feels good and like it. I understand that. He was born tired. The Llama is extremely frank in his social relations. If he doesn't care for you much he makes no effort to conceal his dislike under a conventional smile. He spits in your face. Of course some people can be awfully trying. Occasionally a Llama gets fed up with everything and goes haywire, attacking Peruvians and other animals and acting perfectly horrid. He should not do that. He should count ten. Most Llamas are good mixers. Groups of them will get together behind a mountain to relax and chew the cud and this often leads to much better acquaintance. Young Llamas, or llambs, are born in the spring. Llamas and Alpacas are never seen in a wild state.[5] Guanacos and Vicuñas are always in a wild state. The male Vicuña has from six to fifteen wives. In the mating season two male Vicuñas will often fight until one of them is killed. I guess they don't like each other.

5 Sir Titus Salt (1803-1876) was knighted for making cloth from Alpaca wool, which is better than Llama wool. Queen Victoria loved the stuff.

The Great Anteater

The Great Anteater is a bit on the odd side if you ask me. He lives in Central and South America and looks like something you wouldn't believe. He has a long tubular snout containing a long sticky tongue which he uses in a most peculiar way, and his front claws are so large that he has to walk on the outer edges of his feet to keep from falling all over himself.[1] When the Great Anteater is hungry, he tears into an Ant hill with those huge claws and the Ants come running to the damaged parts of their dwelling to make repairs. Then he captures and swallows them by whipping his tongue in and out of his mouth with great rapidity, two or three times a second. Now really![2] The Great Anteater's bushy tail covers his whole body when he is asleep, so that he resembles a pile of old hay that has been left lying around. He looks a little better that way as you can't see so much. It doesn't seem possible that Great Anteaters would have children but they do. The mother carries Junior on her back for a while and teaches him to stick out his

1 The best animals do not do this.
2 Great Anteaters eat Termites, too. Personally, I hate Termites.

tongue. She throws him out as soon as he starts to look more like Father. The male Great Anteater never goes home to dinner because he knows exactly what he would get. Ants again. Besides, he doesn't want to be tied down. He has a roving eye, so he goes barging around in the tall grass looking for trouble.[3] Why does the Great Anteater look the way he does? Well, I'm afraid that is what comes of eating Ants. Long, long ago, before he had any name, he had begun to live exclusively on Ants and he wanted to become more efficient at it. His one aim through the ages was to be perfectly adapted to the eating of Ants.[4] As Ants are perfectly adapted to being eaten by Anteaters, it all worked out nicely. But the Great Anteater kept right on adding improvements, such as a larger this and a more powerful that, until in my opinion he went too far. There is too much of a build-up. You don't have to be eight feet long in order to eat an Ant and don't try to tell me different. The Tamandua, or Lesser Anteater, is only two feet long and he has no difficulty whatever in eating Ants.[5] The Least Anteater is about the size of a Rat. He would have been enough.

3 Young Anteaters never know their own father — which is just as well, maybe. He's strictly no good.
4 I don't call that much of an ambition. There's no future in it.
5 He can hang by his tail. That makes sense, anyway.

THE YAK

Yaks are supposed to be funny. Some people almost die laughing at the mere thought of a Yak. I feel slightly depressed when I think of a Yak. About one Yak in ten strikes me as funny and he could be funnier. The Yak is a species of Ox[1] indigenous to Tibet and adjacent regions of Central Asia. He has a long, heavy fringe on his sides to show that he is a Yak. This trimming is quaint and old-fashioned but I wouldn't call it so fearfully amusing. It may rate a quiet smile but it is not a belly laugh. It catches dust and dirt and miscellaneous debris, of which there is a great deal in Tibet. The Yak should be sent to the cleaner. Tibetans are crazy about Yaks. They cannot see how other countries manage to get along without these useful animals.[2] Tibetan farmers, or Drokpas, live in yurts or tents made of Yak hair and practice polyandry because there are more men than women in Tibet. When a Drokpa woman has two husbands, one of them tends to the Yak.[3] Tibetans drink

1 Or Cow, as the case may be.
2 They don't.
3 Old Tibetan maxim: Home is where the Yak is.

from thirty to fifty cups of buttered tea every day. This is made of brick tea, parched barley meal, or tsamba, salt, soda, rancid Yak butter, and germs. And they wonder why life seems so futile. Yaks are fine for riding in the Himalayas, if you are not the nervous type. They are apt to throw their loads and they have an odd habit of looking over the edges of cliffs to see what goes on down there. Wild Yaks are really wild. The bulls have hair on their chest a yard long for Yak appeal. They wander around.[4] Old bulls recline on the hillsides and look at the sunset. Yaks have more brawn than brain. They love the frightful sub-zero weather of the Tibetan plateaus. When traveling as a missionary in Tibet in 1846, Abbé Huc passed a herd of fifty Yaks who had been frozen solid to the last Yak while crossing the Tsangpo River. Only their heads were visible above the surface, but he could see through the ice that their legs had been frozen instantaneously in the various correct swimming positions. I hate to be critical, but we all know how one's favorite stories tend to improve. I do believe Abbé Huc saw a Yak who was very, very cold.

4 Wild Yaks charge at high speed and it's no use saying "Nice Yakky! Nice Yakky!" They do not understand English.

THE WART HOG

Consider the Wart Hog. He has bags under his eyes and four tusks in his jaws and large protuberances, or bumps, all over his face. The Wart Hog cannot help it. He was born like that. The way people talk about him, you would think he did it on purpose. The Wart Hog is often called the ugliest of all animals, but the Rhinoceros is uglier because he is larger and there is more of him to be ugly.[1] We should try to forget the Wart Hog's bad points and think of his good ones, only he hasn't any. We cannot say, "After all, he has nice eyes," for that would be a plain, downright falsehood. His eyes are small and shifty and mean-looking. Even if they were wonderful there would still be those bags under them. Yes, the Wart Hog knows he is ugly. You can't look like that and not know it. If people screamed and ran whenever they saw you, wouldn't

1 I have moods when I think the Hippopotamus is ugly. too.

you suspect that something was wrong?[2] Maybe the Wart Hog is not very sensitive. I hope not. I'm afraid nothing much can be done to improve the Wart Hog's appearance.[3] You might work on one or two Wart Hogs for years, but their children would be as ugly as ever, since beauty treatments are not inherited. You would see at a glance that they came of a long line of Wart Hogs.[4] The father and mother Wart Hog do not live together much. Love is blind but not that blind. Sometimes they meet in the forest where the light is more flattering. The late Dr. Crisp of London believed that a cross between the Wart Hog and the Domestic Pig might produce a superior kind of bacon with a streak of fat and a streak of lean all the way through, but he does not seem to have tried it. Dr. Crisp liked his bacon just so.[5] I am sorry to say that the Wart Hog has a nasty disposition. He isn't very bright, either. Yet we can all learn something from him if we observe him closely and meditate upon what we see. The Wart Hog teaches us this useful lesson: Don't be a Wart Hog.

2 In southeastern Africa the Wart Hog is called *Indhlovudawani*, a name which means, "Oh, bother, there's that awful animal again!"
3 A correspondent inquires, "If the Wart Hog would try to think beautiful thoughts all the time, would it help?" No.
4 Infant Wart Hogs resemble both sides of the family.
5 When the King of Ashantee sent Queen Victoria a Wart Hog in 1861, Her Majesty presented it to the Zoo almost instantly. Can you blame her?

Problem
Mammals

❖ ❖ ❖

THE OPOSSUM

The Opussum is a marsupial and marsupials are animals who carry their young around in an abdominal pouch or marsupium.[1] As they have done this for millions and millions of years, they are not likely to stop, no matter how you and I feel about it.[2] Baby Opossums are born in a rudimentary or unfinished state, from four to twenty at once. They are only half an inch long and smaller around than a Honey Bee. This seems hardly worth while, but it suits the mother Opossum, and she is the one directly involved. She thinks the other animals are crazy for having such enormous babies. So she nurses them inside her pouch for two or three months until they reach a reasonable size. During the first two weeks she closes the pouch by means of special Opossum muscles and you wouldn't know there was anything in there. If one of the children comes out before his time she hisses, "You get right back

1 A few marsupials have no abdominal pouch and are therefore hard to identify. If you have one, however, there is no doubt what you are.
2 Opossums go back to the middle of the Upper Cretaceous, would you believe it?

in the marsupium!"[3] Young Opossums are fully developed in a year or so. They have thumbs instead of big toes on their hind feet and not a scrap of morals. The males are just awful. When cornered the Opossum falls on his side and pretends to be dead, hoping the enemy will consider him unfit for food. Some predatory animals do not eat other animals unless they show signs of life. On the other hand, some do. That is the catch in the Opossum's technique. Besides, we all know he is playing possum. Those things get around.[4] Professor Halstead believes Opossums faint from fright and are not really playing possum at all. He states that when they open their eyes they mutter, "Where am I?" The Virginia Opossum is the biggest and best Opossum in the world. He is found in twenty-nine states. Opossums have survived largely because of their arboreal habits. They have lots of fun hanging by their tails and eating persimmons until they almost burst. By and large, there is much to be said for living in trees. Well, it's too late to think of that now.

3 The Opossum language consists of faint hisses, growls and grunts. It is perfectly intelligible to insiders.
4 The Opossum thinks everybody is as dumb as he is — always a dangerous assumption.

THE KANGAROO

Kangaroos live in Australia. They come to this country sometimes, but you can tell at a glance that they do not belong
around here. They carry their young in fur-lined pouches
instead of perambulators.[1] We consider them very primitive in
their notions of anatomy and they think we look awkward with
wheels out in front. It's all in the point of view.[2] All Kangaroo
babies are named Joey. This would not do for us either. We
barely manage to keep things straight as it is, and that would
be the last straw. A Joey is only an inch long at birth. He grows
up in the pouch for four or five months. Then he is supposed to
get out, but sometimes a Joey will stay there even after he has
started a vegetable diet outside and is so large that his mother
can hardly jump. He thinks he owns the place. Anyway, she
knows where he is. He's in the bag.[3] When they are in a hurry
Kangaroos progress by leaps and bounds on their hind legs,
often covering from ten to twenty feet at a time. If they wish to

1 Only the females have pouches.
2 If we wanted pouches, we would have them. Anything's possible these
days.
3 The number of male Kangaroos with an Oedipus complex is surprisingly
small, if that was bothering you. I haven't the statistics right now but I can
assure you there is no cause for alarm.

go slower they hop in a similar way, only not so much so. Someone is always asking why they do this instead of running or walking. They prefer it. The Kangaroo has some good ideas. For instance, he sits on his tail. They can be taught to box, but they have a tendency to use their own rules. A favorite blow is a stiff uppercut to the solar plexus with the left hind foot. They have been known to display quite a sense of humor with their keeper and chance acquaintances. Whenever a Kangaroo puts his paws on your shoulder and gives you a big grin, that is the time to leave. The Kangaroo was discovered in 1770 by Captain James Cook, who was a great one for going to foreign lands and inquiring into the habits and customs of the people.[4] When Captain Cook asked the natives of Australia the name of the strange creature, they replied "*Kan-ga-roo*," and he wrote it down in his notebook. It is possible, of course, that "*Kan-ga-roo*" in the aboriginal language meant, "Oh, go away and shut up!"[5] It turned out all right in the end, because any other name for the Kangaroo would sound just silly.

4 The marsupial seen by William Dampier in 1699 was only a Banded Hare Wallaby.

5 A few years later Captain Cook was slain with a blunt instrument while asking questions in the Sandwich Islands.

THE KOALA

The Koala or Native Bear of Australia is not a bear. He is a marsupial, but he wants to look like a Teddy Bear and he succeeds so well that most people think he is one.[1] Koalas are quaint little creatures with woolly gray fur and an expression of utter innocence. Nobody is as innocent as all that. I wasn't born yesterday. The truth is that Koalas are polygamous and most of them are promiscuous. Koalas live in eucalyptus trees, sleeping by day in some comfortable fork of their dwelling and eating the leaves at night. This sounds like an ideal existence, but it isn't quite perfect. You finally run out of leaves and have to move to another tree. Koalas subsist entirely upon eucalyptus leaves and will eat only twelve of the 380 species found in Australia. If you offer them some other kind they say it's spinach. In a state of nature they never drink any water. When offered a spoonful of the stuff, they try to chew it. In captivity they learn to drink sweetened tea and eat cake and die of indigestion. They are subject to pneumonia, ophthalmic

1 Teddy Bears are bona fide Bears without abdominal pouches or any such nonsense.

diseases, periostitis of the skull, internal parasites, and ticks.[2] The male Koala is neurotic. During the mating season from early September to late January he sits on a limb and wails all night long, stopping only for meals. When crossed in love he screams something awful, but he soon forgets the incident and resumes his soft melancholy cry. Koalas cannot remember for more than ten minutes, the lucky fellows![3] You can't own a Koala because they are now so scarce that they are not allowed to leave Australia. Maybe it's just as well, for pet Koalas are really something. They hate to be left alone and take steps to prevent it. They fasten their arms around your neck and hold on until forcibly detached. They also hang to your clothing by all their sharp little claws and cannot be induced to let go of your hair. You spend most of your time picking Koalas off yourself. Koalas are at their best in their favorite pick-a-back position. Mother and child are simply adorable as they look out from their tree, full-face view,

2 Koalas have no tails and their vermiform appendix is six to eight feet in length. Odd, to say the least.
3 I'd tell you more, but I seldom spend the night up a eucalyptus tree.

watching for someone to show up with a camera. Koalas are so gentle that they never attack anybody and they cannot defend themselves because they wouldn't have the slightest idea how to do it.[4] I really don't see how they are going to get along, the way things are nowadays.

4 If you pinch a fullgrown Koala ever so gently, he just sits down and cries.

THE TASMANIAN WOLF

The Tasmanian Wolf lives far, far away on the other side of the world, thank goodness. As they kill and eat Sheep whenever they get a chance, most of the Tasmanian Wolves have been shot by the other Tasmanians and the rest have been driven into wild, mountainous regions where there aren't any Sheep. They do not like this but they do the best they can with the material at hand. They will settle for almost anything.[1] Tasmanian Wolves look and act much like other Wolves, but wait till you hear. They are not really Wolves at all.[2] They are marsupials. Even the male Tasmanian Wolf has a functionless rudimentary pouch, or marsupium, and he expects to be taken seriously! Although he seldom attacks people, the Tasmanian Wolf can be most annoying. He will follow you at some little distance or sit down in front of you and leer in a rather fright-

[1] At some seasons of the year they are seen prowling along the seashore in search of prey. Up to no good, as usual.
[2] If you behave like a Wolf, you will soon resemble one.

ening manner. If you ignore him completely he may go away, but he is more than likely to show up again at the next corner, leer and all. He thinks he is smooth. When excited, the Tasmanian Wolf utters a short, guttural cough or loud wheeze. He cannot howl or whistle.[3] He can't wag his tail, either.[4] If you are not sure what kind of animal you are dealing with, observe him closely when he turns around. He is a Tasmanian Wolf all right if he has from sixteen to eighteen dark transverse stripes on his lower back. It is often necessary to be firm with Tasmanian Wolves. Some years ago, when they were all over the place, one of these creatures boldly entered the cottage of Mr. Blinkworth, a Tasmanian farmer, and ran after his young daughter, snapping at her repeatedly, but missing. Mr. Blinkworth, entering at this point, seized the intruder by the tail, swung him over his head, and dashed him to the floor with all his might. And that was the last of *that* Tasmanian Wolf.

3 Some Wolf!
4 See Professor Pfungst on the Wolf, only he's not very funny.

THE BANDICOOT

Bandicoots are smallish marsupials inhabiting Australia, Tasmania, and New Guinea. They are interesting in a mild way but a little weak in the head. For one thing, they have their abdominal pouches on backwards, with the opening at the wrong end. You may wonder why the babies don't keep falling out all the time. They do. The force of gravity functions over there, too. The worst of it is that Bandicoot mothers spring into the air when disturbed and they are always jumping around for no reason, so the children never know where they are. Bandicoots will have to stop this or become extinct. They seem to realize that all is not as it should be, so the more thoughtful ones get together about every million years and decide to change the length of their ears. Thus we have many species of Bandicoots with different ear measurements and pouches that are still upside down. They haven't noticed that yet. The Bilby or Rabbit Bandicoot[1] has enormous ears and a self-satisfied smirk on his face.[2] He thinks he is getting by as

1 Formerly called the Jecko or Wuirrapur.
2 His ears are three and a half inches long and two and one-twelfth inches wide at the base. His tarsus measures only twenty-one twenty-fourths of an inch.

44

a Rabbit but he is not fooling me for one moment.[3] He is easy to identify, but if you are looking for a Mountain Bandicoot, a species recognizable by its moderately large ears, you might have trouble, as there is some doubt about what constitutes moderately large ears in a Bandicoot. You have to carry a lot of sample Bandicoots of standard ear size with you for purposes of comparison and striking an average.[4] Even then you may overlook a genuine Mountain Bandicoot who happens to have outsize ears like his grandfather's. Bandicootology has certain drawbacks as a career. Bandicoots are hard to bring into the conversation and harder to keep there.[5] One can knock oneself out measuring Bandicoots' ears from the cradle to the grave, practically, and who cares, I mean *really*? Besides, there is the danger that a Bandicootologist may get a somewhat distorted view. I have spells when I wonder whether everything can be explained in terms of Bandicoots' ears, and then again I am not at all sure that it can't. Sometimes I wish I had never heard of Bandicoots.[6]

3 Rabbits have much shorter noses and tails and they aren't eternally grinning.
4 These should include a Bilby for one extreme and a Southern Short-faced Bandicoot, whose ear is only two-thirds of an inch long — definitely shortish.
5 In my opinion the art of conversation is doomed.
6 I have been asked to explain the sex life of the Bandicoot. They travel in pairs, if that answers the question.

THE WOMBAT

If you know nothing whatever about the Wombat, this would be a good piece to read. It might come in handy some time. There are people who go around asking about Wombats and you may run into one of them yet. "Why are Wombats found only in Australia and Tasmania?" is one of their questions. Answer: Because that is the way things are arranged. They also ask, "Why are Wombats?" Wombats would call that one just foolish. They feel that if there is going to be anything at all, there must be Wombats. They set great store by the fact that they are the only animals on earth who are Wombats. They would not dream of being anything else and they certainly wouldn't want to be us. It has never occurred to a Wombat that as a marsupial he is almost as low as a monotreme[1] and that we belong to the Primates, an order of mammals including the Apes, Monkeys, Marmosets, and Lemurs. We even have a family name, *Hominidae*, to distinguish us, tech-

---

[1] A monotreme is a mammal that lays eggs. You can't get any lower.

nically, from Gibbons, Chimpanzees, Orangutans, and Gorillas.[2] The Wombat has a chunky physique, short legs, and a generally uncouth and frowsy look. Some think he resembles a much overgrown Woodchuck. The truth is, he looks like nothing much. The average Wombat is about a yard long from the tip of his nose to his vestigial tail. The Giant Wombat of the Pleistocene was as large as a Rhinoceros. This was obviously too much Wombat and he was discontinued. The Common or Naked-nosed Wombat of southeastern Australia is the largest and most uninteresting of living Wombats. Tasmanian Wombats have tough hides and thick, coarse hair. They lead extremely boresome lives. Then they are made into rugs or doormats. And you think you have troubles.[3] Pet Wombats occasionally show some signs of affection, if you need it that

2 It has been suggested that Wombats are unnecessary because they haven't much sense. There's a laugh in that somewhere, if I had time to work on it.
3 The Common Wombat and the Tasmanian Wombat are said to have fifteen pairs of ribs to thirteen for the Southern Hairy-nosed Wombat and the Queensland Hairy-nosed Wombat. I see no reason to doubt this.

much. They bite you from time to time in a listless manner and for no reason that is apparent to a non-Wombat. Always remember that Wombats are nocturnal burrowing animals.[4] If you have them indoors, they keep you awake all night trying to burrow through the floor. If you let them out, they have a tendency to undermine the foundations of the house. Some rather sad accidents have happened that way.[5] Now you know more about Wombats than you did before. Oh, you do so!

[4] Wombats are remotely descended from a tree-dwelling animal. Well, I'm the last one to hold that against them.
[5] The original human inhabitants of Tasmania gave up long ago and became extinct, but the Wombat goes right on trying, at least in April, May, and June. They have only one Wombat at a time.

THE POET AND THE NAUTILUS

If I am a little weak on any one thing, it is probably the Greek poets. Yet I feel that I must say a few words about Callimachus, who lived in the third century B.C. and left behind him some lines on the Chambered Nautilus, as we now call this interesting little animal, familiar enough to most of us from the much better poem by Oliver Wendell Holmes. Trifling — indeed, perfectly silly — as Callimachus' verses may be, he was first in the field (so far as I know) and I think it most unfair that his name is always omitted from articles on natural history, even those purporting to deal in a comprehensive way with the Cephalopoda, or head-footed mollusks.

Although the dates on Callimachus are somewhat sketchy, it seems fairly clear that in 280 B.C., at the invitation of Ptolemy II, later known as Ptolemy Philadelphus, who was doubtless impressed by the man's reputation as the leading grammarian of his day, he became head of the library at Alexandria, succeeding Zenodotus of Ephesus, a critic and editor famous for subjecting the Homeric texts to numerous changes which had to be changed back again by later critics and editors. He was followed in this position, and a very good one it was, too, by Eratosthenes of Cyrene, founder of astronomical geography and a powerful influence upon such scholars as Poseidonius, Strabo and Claudius Ptolemaeus, the last mentioned of whom assigned latitude and longitude to every important place on the habitable globe, all quite incorrectly.

Of his eight hundred works, says the *Encyclopaedia Britannica* in its article on Callimachus, only six hymns, sixty-four epigrams and various fragments are extant. For instance, as I learned in Mr. Whibley's excellent *A Companion to Greek Studies*, a book I once happened to buy when I was out of my depth on some other classical subject, certain fragments were discovered at Oxyrhynchus in 1905 and published five years later. Among other items, they restored to us the last part of the love story of Acontius and Cydippe, apparently a harmless enough tale of its kind, if only we had more of the plot, and the final book of the *Aitia*, in which the author forswears poetry and resolves to stick to prose for the future, a promise he may or may not have kept. As it turned out, 1910 was a bad year for Callimachus fragments, and they failed to catch on.

A complete appraisal of Callimachus as grammarian, librarian and undisputed boss of the Alexandrian literary set for forty years or more cannot be made here. Perhaps his supreme achievement was his *Pinaces*, a catalogue of the library with critical and biographical comments in a hundred and twenty volumes, one of the longest documents of the kind ever produced. His energy, even in old age, in putting down writers whose papyri contained split infinitives and dangling participles, if you can do that in Greek, is said to have discouraged all but the hungriest aspirants to fame. Besides, you had to agree with Callimachus about everything under the sun before you could hope to be in. If not, you were decidedly out.

This may be the place to mention Callimachus' celebrated

quarrel with Apollonius of Rhodes, his former pupil, an affair which profoundly shook the Greek literary world, especially Apollonius. The two had never seen eye to eye on certain matters, and the rift widened when, after the publication of Apollonius' *Argonautica*, an epic poem in four books, Callimachus came out with a Greek proverb to the effect that some books are a little too long. Well, it rankled.

It seems that Apollonius, though a much younger man, had worked after the old models, such as Homer, a procedure repugnant to Callimachus, who had picked up the idea somewhere that an author's writings should always be integrated in the life of his own times, as he put it. He kept repeating this so often that Apollonius, driven to the verge of a nervous breakdown, told him in so many words that it was not only a vile phrase but a feeble-minded cliché directly responsible for most of the trash turned out in Alexandria and duly exhibited at the library, meaning nothing personal. I really have no documentary proof of the exact wordage. It's my contribution, if that is the right word.

The details of the feuding have not come down to us as fully as might be wished, but anyone who is even slightly acquainted with the literary temperament can supply the missing links. Things would seem to be going along all right between the two until, one day, Apollonius would remark, offhand and naming no names, that it was a pity some epigrams did not seem to ep. Callimachus would say yes, and it was a downright crime, in view of the slim supply of papyrus, that some epic poems in four books had not been issued in the only form their style and content would appear to warrant, as short shorts.

If I know my grammarians, there would also be sessions at which the most frightful allegations of a non-literary nature would be tossed back and forth, some of them, I fear, only too true. Since scandal in the third century B.C. had to be really awful to register at all, Callimachus must finally have raked up something unusually fiendish, for Apollonius suddenly withdrew to Rhodes; or, as we of today would say, he got out of town.

I must be brief in my estimate of the main body of Calli-machus' surviving work, based upon a hasty reading of it in a volume which a kindly librarian slipped to me overnight. (After all, one can't take weeks and weeks to do this sort of thing.) The encyclopaedia agrees with me that the hymns to Zeus, Apollo, Artemis and so forth are "extremely learned, and written in a laboured style, unrelieved by poetic genius." I shall not add a word to that. It's perfect just as it stands. Some of the epigrams aren't half bad, if you don't mind char-acters who seem to have limited their activities pretty consis-tently to impairing one another's morals in this way or that. I was rather pleased to learn that Callimachus had his enthusi-asms, such as they were. I didn't think it was in him.

Anyhow, he kept right at it, turning out copy, hanging on to his job, and scaring everybody speechless until, to the great relief of all and sundry, he finally died in 240 B.C. An apoc-ryphal anecdote has it that when the news was brought to Apollonius as he stood on the shore at Rhodes, gazing sea-ward, he remarked: "This comes as a shock to me. I thought the old bastard would live forever."

And now, if I have sufficiently aroused your interest in the poet, let us turn to the poem, an English version of which by an unknown hand (at least to me) I happened to find in an old volume that was knocking around the house. Originally in twelve lines, but running to eighteen in this translation, it amounts to a graceful little speech by the shell of a Nautilus upon its dedication by a young woman from Smyrna to the goddess Zephyrites, as she is here called.

I'm afraid I am a little shaky on my Graeco-Egyptian deities, too, but Zephyrites appears to be, as near as I can make out from the reference works at hand, nobody but our friend Aphrodite in a rather outlandish guise. For she is at one and the same time, if I can believe my ears, Arsinoë II, the sister and second wife of this Ptolemy Philadelphus who gave Callimachus his job at the library — and wouldn't that notable hand-kisser be just the old party to be getting in right with the lady? It seems she received divine honors — and mind you, she was still alive — at various temples, including one at Zephyrium, where she was worshipped as Arsinoë Aphrodite, patroness of all sea-farers, such as sailors, passengers, and Nautilus shells. The nerve of her!

Anyhow, the poem begins:

A sacred shell, Zephyrites divine,
Fair Silenœa offers at thy shrine;
And thus thy Nautilus is doubly blest,
Since given by her, and still by thee possest.

So far so good. I like that. Best of all, I understand it. The shell proceeds:

Of late, small tackling from my body grew,
Thin sails I spread when winds propitious blew;
But when the seas were calm, to gain the shores,
I stretched my little feet, like lab'ring oars,
And, from my busy limbs and painted side,
Was called a Polyp, as I stemmed the tide;
Till driven by winds on Coan rocks I shone,
And now recline before Arsinoë's throne.
Depriv'd of life, no more on seas I rest,
Or draw young Halcyons from the watery nest;
But be this boon to Clinea's daughter given:
A virtuous maid, and fav'rite of high heaven;
The precious boon may Silenœa gain,
When she from Smyrna ploughs the watery main.

I confess I had to get help on this final part of the poem, especially the line about drawing young Halcyons from their watery nest, a bit of Nautilus lore with which I was unfamil-

53

iar, up to my neck as I am in the rest of it. Fortunately, I asked a superman, that is, a person who reads Greek; for it soon developed that in the original the Nautilus shell says, in a sad sort of way, that no longer, since he is dead, will the eggs of the Halcyon, or Kingfisher, be laid in his chambers, as when he was alive. Amazing what these people know who had sense enough to study in their youth. In my day, if you took Greek you were a greasy grind, only a notch or two above a Phi Beta Kappa, and now I'm paying for it.

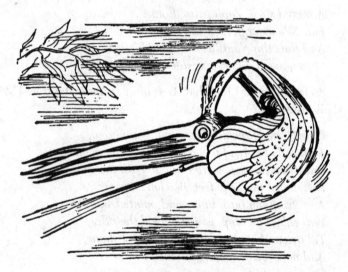

My point is that if the Nautilus of the story had chambers in his shell, as the shell clearly states, then he was a Chambered, or Pearly, Nautilus, as distinguished from the Argonaut, or Paper Nautilus, a different kind of Cephalopod with which he is often confused. There is really no doubt about it, unless my learned helper erred in translating one of Callimachus' words — which one I wouldn't know — as "chambers," and I see no reason why he should do so. I should think it would be rather difficult, if not impossible, to translate a Greek word as "chambers," unless it actually *was* chambers. *Chambers* is not a word one keeps handy for use in faking translations — it's too special a word. That's only one man's opinion, but I'm sticking to it. I mention it only because certain commentators have identified our little cephalopod as a Paper Nautilus and they are sure to be furious with me for begging to differ. Well, they could be wrong.

Of course no Kingfisher in its right mind would venture into the outer chamber, inhabited as it is by a little beast so ugly as the Chambered Nautilus, who, for that matter, fills every inch of it himself and spills over outside. Thirdly, Kingfishers do not lay eggs in the Chambered Nautilus. Or in the Paper Nautilus, either.

I cannot name the source of Callimachus' Halcyon data at the moment, but I think I see where he stole his ideas about the sails and the oars. From Aristotle, of course. Who else starts all these stories? Who but he would have a mind powerful enough to think them up? Aristotle said it a hundred years before, about the Argonaut, or Paper Nautilus, and it is utter rot, since the Paper Nautilus does not sail or row any more than the Chambered Nautilus does. Both push themselves backwards by ejecting water from a siphon, or funnel, in the head-foot, like the rest of the Cephalopoda or head-footed mollusks. I happen to know that for a fact.

Thus Callimachus got it from Aristotle and the Nautilus of the poem got it from Callimachus, you might say. Callimachus had only to appropriate a piece of ignorant gibberish from a book by somebody who didn't know what he was talking about, hang it on the wrong animal altogether and see that it rhymed, and there he was, practically in the Loeb Classical Library. But what about the poor Nautilus, compelled as the poet's creature to spout what he must have known to be a string of manifest untruths about himself and his species? If ever I saw a mollusk in a false position, he's it. One can only hope that he was content to play it that way since he was all washed up on Coan's shore anyhow, so what did he have to lose?

The Aristotelian reference is to be found in his *Historia Animalium*, sandwiched in between other erroneous matter about the Argonaut's method of rising and sinking in the water by emptying and filling its shell. After describing what he regards. as a certain web-growth between its tentacles, he states: "It uses this structure, when a breeze is blowing, for a sail, and lets down some of its feelers alongside as rudder-oars." Wrong, all wrong. Terribly, terribly wrong.

It was this passage which Pliny the Elder, in the first century of the Christian era, rendered in somewhat more picturesque terms, thus: "This fish [*sic*], in order to rise to the surface, turns upon his back and heaves himself up little by little; to swim with more ease he discharges all the water within him (bilgewater, as it were) from a pipe. After this, turning up his two fore claws or arms he displays and stretches between them a membrane or skin of a wonderful thinness." Bilge-water is right. He has his sexes badly mixed up too, as we shall see.

"This," Pliny proceeds, "serves him instead of a sail in the air above water. With the rest of his arms or claws he rows and labors under water, and with his tail directs his course and steers as it were with a helm. Thus he makes his way in the sea with a fair show of a foist, or galley, under sail."

In a word, to hear Aristotle and his disciples tell it, the Paper Nautilus can do almost anything in the way of seamanship except cry "Aye, aye, sir!" and call for a noggin of rum. It is true that the Paper Nautilus is sometimes seen at the surface of the ocean, putt-putting backwards by a somewhat dated kind of jet propulsion, but the Chambered Nautilus stays on or near the bottom, swimming in the same fashion, crawling on the ocean floor with his head-foot, or jerking himself along the rocks by his ninety tentacles in search of Shrimps and other crustaceans. He never comes to the surface unless he is dead or dying, in which condition he resembles a much damaged Tortoise-shell Cat. That's the thing to look for.

I must admit, in fairness to all concerned, that two of the eight arms of the Paper Nautilus are expanded into flat membranous plates at the end and that a person that way disposed might interpret these as fore gaff topsails or the like without finding himself certified as a dangerous lunatic. Aristotle did, as we have seen. But get this. The Paper Nautilus clasps these two arms tightly around her papery shell to keep it in repair, for it is secreted from the membraneous plates, and to prevent her eggs from falling out, not to mention herself. Since she is not attached to the shell in any other way, she would be in a fine fix if she ever relaxed her grip by mistake, as she would go her way and the shell would go its, with highly embarrassing results. For this last observation I am indebted to certain remarks made by the late Dr. Andrew Wilson, F.R.S.E., some years ago before the Sunday Lecture Society, Newcastle-upon-Tyne.

Still and all, the female Argonaut is reported to leave her shell occasionally to look for food, but only when she is sure she can return to it to protect her family. At such times she fares quite as well in the water as the male of the species, who is completely naked and only one-fifteenth her size, poor fellow. When disturbed or annoyed, she is likely to pop out of her shell and swim away, regardless of consequences, as one did when Dr. William Beebe was looking her over on his *Arcturus* voyage. A nasty little witch she was, too, flouncing about in a fearful temper and trying to squirt ink on so kindly an investigator as Dr. Beebe, imagine!

There's a scientist, now, who will never be caught running down Aristotle, come what may. I recall some of his tributes to the sage, so rich in feeling and in reason that the memory almost persuades me I have been a fool to spend so much of my time and energy in fighting what I take to be the old fellow's pernicious influence on art, letters, science and sundry. Reading one of Dr. Beebe's pages again, I am softened enough to grant that, for all I know, Aristotle may well have been the smartest man who ever lived — up to that time, if I may say so at some slight risk of being misunderstood.

So rabid an Aristotle fan, indeed, is Dr. Beebe (who, by the way, is an authority on the Argonaut, or Paper Nautilus) that he only reluctantly confesses that his hero is cockeyed on the animal's sailing propensities. Having noted the mistake, does he then rave and carry on as a less gentle scientist might be tempted to do when he has spotted an error? No, he just writes some more about "the founder of natural history and the greatest naturalist of all time." It is not that Dr. Beebe is making allowances for Aristotle. He really admires the man. But where were we?

Frankly, I had intended at this juncture to trace the employment of the Nautilus as a poetic device in all languages, dead or alive, since 384 B.C., the date of Aristotle's birth. I have suddenly decided, however, for one reason or another, to confine myself to a few examples in a language I speak myself, a more modest undertaking but one which may clear up a few stray points about the anatomy, habitat, sex life and mental equipment of our English and American poets. Take Alexander Pope, who sings:

> For thus to man the voice of Nature spake:
> Go, from the creatures thy instruction take;
> Learn of the little Nautilus to sail,
> Spread the thin oar, and catch the driving gale.

These lines, not unreminiscent of Oppian, who opined that the Nautilus served as a model for the man who invented ships and promoted ocean travel, may strike you as more cogent if you are willing to assume that going nowhere backwards constitutes the art of navigation. Perhaps no further comment is needed on this little passage by the great eighteenth-century poet. Its place in literature is obvious to one and all.

Or listen to Wordsworth:

Spread, tiny nautilus, the living sail,
Dive at thy choice, or brave the freshening gale.
If unreprov'd the ambitious eagle mount
Sunward, to seek the daylight in its fount,
Bays, gulf, and ocean's Indian widths shall be
Till the world perishes a field for thee.

At first glance it is hard to see what is going on here. A second reading convinces one that it is what one suspected, a Nautilus taking a trip to the sun on the back of an eagle, or having the idea put into his head, anyhow. The catch is that such a venture would be highly dangerous for the Nautilus. I can't speak for the Paper Nautilus, but the eye of the Chambered Nautilus consists of an open pit with no lens, and the surface of the retina must be bathed constantly with sea water in order to function. He can see well enough in the ocean depths where he belongs, but on an eagle he would be totally blind and probably fall off and hurt himself before you could say Cephalopoda Tetrabranchiata. I was warned in school that Wordsworth had his dull moments.

Enter Lord Byron with a male Paper Nautilus maneuvering a canoe he does not possess and could not manage in any case, as follows:

The tender Nautilus who steers his prow,
The sea-born sailor of the shell canoe,
The ocean Mab, the fairy of the sea,
Seems far less fragile, and alas! more free.

More free than what or from what I couldn't say, as my sample of Byron consists only of these lines. The Nautilus certainly doesn't seem to be free from gross misrepresentation and gratuitous insult, what with Lord Byron going out of his

59

way to call him an ocean Mab. Nothing could be farther from the facts or more unfair to this manly little mollusk, as everybody knows who takes the trouble to study his detachable third left arm, a member specially modified for what he has in mind. The male Paper Nautilus is a perfectly respectable husband and father, Lord Byron, if you see what I mean.

Which brings me to my final exhibit, "The Chambered Nautilus" by our own beloved Oliver Wendell Holmes, a poem which is of course a must for any Nautilus article, from its first lines, remember?

> This is the ship of pearl, which, poets feign,
>> Sails the unshadowed main, —
>> The venturous bark that flings
> On the sweet summer wind its purpled wings,
> In gulfs enchanted, where the Siren sings,
>> And coral reefs lie bare,
> Where the cold sea-maids rise to sun their streaming hair.

I trust you get the full effect of those key words, "which, poets feign." They show that Dr. Holmes, well aware of the true facts about the Chambered Nautilus, as he certainly was, is only playing along with the fable for a starter. They also hold out the promise that once Dr. Holmes has finished his fraternal bow to Callimachus and the rest he will give us something very different from this classic applesauce, something more in accord with the findings of Rumphius, the great Dutch physician and botanist who first described and figured the Chambered Nautilus with a fair degree of accuracy in 1705, from observations made during his long residence at Amboyna. I often think we would all be better off if we paid less attention to Aristotle and more to Rumphius.

We now gather, in the last two lines of feigning, that the Nautilus, too, is no more. We have another dead Nautilus on our hands, only the shell of his former self, a shell we are pretty sure is not going to tell us a pack of ridiculous lies.

Its webs of living gauze no more unfurl;
Wrecked is the ship of pearl!
And every chambered cell
Where its dim dreaming life was wont to dwell,
As the frail tenant shaped his growing shell
Before thee lies revealed,—
Its irised ceiling rent, its sunless crypt unsealed!

Since the shell is evidently in median section, as we sometimes see them in shops and museums, it may be interesting (to the right parties) to note what Dr. Holmes omits mentioning for some reason, that the various cells, or chambers, are connected by a siphuncle, a slender tubular prolongation of the visceral hump which runs through them all and is believed to provide them with a gas containing more nitrogen, or perhaps one should say less oxygen, than exists in atmospheric air, to maintain a correct pressure and make the heavy shell more buoyant. Period.

I recall in this connection that the Chambered Nautilus caught by Mr. H. N. Moseley of H.M.S. *Challenger*, while dredging off Makutu Island in 320 fathoms, shed little or no light on the gas business. Mr. Moseley had him swimming round and round in a shallow tub and, to tell the truth, that's about all that happened. He (the Nautilus) was expected to submerge from time to time but failed to do so, whether because of some injury to his siphuncle or a disinclination to sink in a few inches of water, or what, we shall never know. Mr. Mosely thought maybe he had the bends, as is quite possible.

A few observers have disputed the whole gas theory on the ground that an animal full of gas would not be able to stay down. Personally, I feel that the Nautilus could take care of that detail without too much trouble. If he has this gas apparatus at all, and I believe he has, he must know how to run it. On the other hand, Mr. George Bennett, M.R.C.S., F.L.S., who opened a specimen at sea in 1832, reported it to contain sea water but no gas, and a Professor Woodward, as of 1870, breaking into one preserved in spirits of wine, found in the chambers what appeared to be some liquid of an alcoholic nature.

Since it would be murder to omit Dr. Holmes' third stanza — or any of his poem for that matter — we may now refresh our memory on the main activity of the Chambered Nautilus, his building and moving operations, which are to figure largely from there on. Let's have it, without further ado.

> Year after year beheld the silent toil
>   That spread his lustrous coil;
>   Still, as the spiral grew,
> He left the past year's dwelling for the new,
> Stole with soft step its shining archway through,
>   Built up its idle door,
> Stretched in his last-found home, and knew the old
>   no more.

Here one begins to see that the poet is leading up to something having to do with a single aspect of his subject, the one

we have just noticed. He would have gained nothing to his purpose by telling us that the coiled bilaterally symmetrical calcareous shell of the Chambered Nautilius, including the septa, or partitions, is secreted by the mantle, that the anterior portion of the head-foot is modified to form an operculum or lid to the whole shebang, or that the Chambered Nautilus possesses no ink sac, as do all the other Cephalopoda except the Tetrabranchiata.

We see, too — or rather we feel it in our bones — that Dr. Holmes is about to draw a lesson from the life of the Chambered Nautilus. It will be a fine lesson, and I shall quote it in a jiffy for the good it may do those who need it, though I cannot honestly say — my conscience simply will not let me — that the Chambered Nautilus is an ideal animal upon whom to base a sermon, uplifting as that sermon may be if you can forget what inspired it. The Cephalopoda, to which the Chambered Nautilus belongs, are generally regarded as the highest kind of invertebrates and real prodigies among the mollusks (look at the Clam, for instance — there's a dumb one for you), but I do feel strongly that there is still room for improvement.

Unhappily the Chambered Nautilus is one of the least intelligent if not the very stupidest of the cephalopods, most of whom, like the Octopus and the Squid, long since discarded their heavy external shells, thereby procuring for themselves increased agility and many other advantages that we all need if we are to get around and see the world with a reasonable degree of comfort and efficiency. External shells were all right in Paleozoic times or even in the earlier stages of the Mesozoic, but it couldn't last and the Cephalopoda knew it. The brighter among them went in for internal skeletons or quietly gave up after a more or less prolonged struggle for existence. Struggle is said to be good for the constitution, but enough's enough.

Worse and more of it, the shell of the Chambered Nautilus is one of the clumsiest on record, with all those unused chambers adding to its weight and unwieldiness, but somehow he stuck it out and is still to be found in dwindling numbers in a small area of the Indian Ocean between the Fiji and Philippine Islands. All the other cephalopods with external shells, including the powerful Ammonites, became extinct when their time was up, and scientists have long wondered why he didn't follow their example. My own guess would be that he hadn't that much sense.

For 550 million years the Chambered Nautilus has been building and moving and dragging around with him all the old apartments he has ever lived in, and for what? All he gets out of it, so far as I can see, is the dubious distinction of being the only existing cephalopod with an external chambered shell and occasional mention as a living fossil in some learned publication. And what use is he, anyway, except to the Fiji Islanders? They eat him, when they can't get anything else. Properly prepared, he tastes not unlike a piece of old chenille curtain.

Please note that any nasty cracks I may have made while reviewing "The Chambered Nautilus" were directed at the animal rather than at Oliver Wendell Holmes. I stress this because of a little talk I had the other day with a scientific friend, a Nautilus expert, among other things, whose first name also happens to be Will, like Dr. Beebe and me. I was hardly launched on my critical exposition when I caught a look in his bright blue eyes that struck me — well, it struck me. Since it is not in the man's nature to be unkind, I don't say that his look meant what I feared at the moment it *might* mean. I only say that in someone else that look *could* have meant that it was hardly likely, but that just possibly Oliver Wendell Holmes was as bright as I am.

At that moment I resolved to go easy on Dr. Holmes, even if I should find flagrant errors in his iambic pentameters and Alexandrines — which, by the way, I did not. Rather than displease Dr. William K. Gregory, for it was he, I would scrap a hundred articles, God forbid, but surely he will forgive me if, in a much chastened spirit, I set down the rest of the poem and conclude with one or two purely personal reactions which have nothing to do with science. The awful part of it is that I'm afraid he loves the Chambered Nautilus too. Thus Dr. Holmes:

> *Thanks for the heavenly message brought by thee,*
> > *Child of the wandering sea,*
> > *Cast from her lap, forlorn!*
> *From thy dead lips a clearer note is born*
> *Than ever Triton blew from wreathèd horn!*
> > *While on mine ear it rings,*
> *Through the deep caves of thought I heard a voice that*
> > *sings—*
>
> *Build thee more stately mansions, O my soul,*
> > *As the swift seasons roll!*
> > *Leave thy low-vaulted past!*
> *Let each new temple, nobler than the last,*
> *Shut thee from heaven with a dome more vast,*
> > *Till thou at length art free,*
> *Leaving thine outgrown shell by life's unresting sea!*

There you are, and now I wonder what ever gave me the mad idea of taking Dr. Holmes and his poem apart, as I once promised myself that I would? Had I forgotten that finally I must come to those grand last stanzas, where my mild, harmless heckling would sound just plain foolish? Or what? Why does one do these perfectly idiotic things? Why was I ever born? There's a question for you.

It was probably that remark about my soul that set me off. I don't think of it as low-vaulted, especially. My past was fair enough, as those things go in this world. I convinced myself of that years ago by mental and moral gymnastics that I wouldn't want to go through again even if I had the strength, and I'm not going to back down at this stage of the game. If Dr. Holmes includes my present, too, and I gather he does, the same line of reasoning holds good.

I guess I'm sensitive about my soul. Seems to me it isn't too terrible, surely not in need of any complete overhauling and repair job. I've kept it in mind all along. I won't say it has steadily grown in grace year by year, because I don't believe as much as that was wrong with it in the first place. My soul in early youth was certainly as good as it is now, if not better, and come to think of it I shouldn't wonder if Dr. Holmes had something to do with that pleasant state of affairs. As I strode

up and down our back yard shouting parts of "The Chambered Nautilus" at the top of my voice, first in order to learn the words by heart and thus retain my standing as teacher's pet, later for the joy of showing off a bit, I don't recall that I thought very deeply about the meaning of it all. I just liked it. Anyway, it couldn't have harmed me and maybe it helped. Maybe it sank in.

As for those more stately mansions of the soul that Dr. Holmes so beautifully recommends, I am not absolutely sure that I qualify there. It doesn't sound like me. I just go along doing the best I can, but nothing too wonderful, nothing sensational. Not that I haven't laid plans for larger mansions than I have achieved. Again and again I did that. I tried. I might have succeeded, too, if I hadn't been crossed up every time by persons I can only describe as lowdown rats — and that's too good for them. If I haven't quite made the grade you can blame them for it, don't blame me.

What it boils down to, probably, is that I don't like to be pushed around by a Chambered Nautilus. I am simply not a candidate for sudden reform by the most primitive of existing Cephalopoda. I am willing to learn, but I can't see myself sitting at the head-foot of a living fossil who is only one jump ahead of total extinction because of his numerous and ineradicable faults. Besides, take a look at him. His pictures may not do him justice, but I have never seen an uglier little beast in all my life, pretty as his shell may be when polished and stuck on the mantel-piece. In a word, if I wanted a model to follow in thought or deed, it would not be the likes of *him*.

PLEASURES
OF POND LIFE

❖   ❖   ❖

THE FROG

The Frog is a vertebrate of the class Amphibia and he doesn't even know it. He just lives in the water and on land and lets it go at that.[1] Frogs are studied in high schools and colleges to see what makes them jump. I suppose there has been progress in this direction since I took Frogology One. I hope so. You can't get much firsthand information on that point because the Frog himself doesn't know how he does it.[2] As with other animals I could mention, the Frog's brain issues orders to the rest of the nervous system and then he does whatever he pleases. Frogs are lower vertebrates, so they go right on making the same old mistakes over and over, regardless of all the trouble it brings them. Higher vertebrates check on their actions most carefully and profit by experience. Now you tell one. A hypnotized Frog will lie perfectly motionless in your hand, some-

1 The Frog has no ribs. A fine sort of vertebrate!
2 "A decapitated Frog responds less readily to external stimuli." — Walbridge.

times for hours, with his arms and legs in the air and a foolish grin on his face. I forget what this teaches. Frogology One was all right but I often wish we had studied some brighter animal.[3] The Frog is by far our best croaker. His peculiar vocal method enables him to croak both coming and going. Other croakers cannot hope to equal him, as they have to stop for breath. Oddly enough, male Frogs croak more than the females. The croaking of the Bullfrog has been compared to the bellowing of a Bull. This may be true of a very large Bullfrog and a very small Bull.[4] At the opening of the spring social season, all the male Frogs of the pond assemble on the bank and render "Sweet Adeline." Then they join the ladies in the water for a program of swimming events. The rest of the year is rather dull for Frogs, but they have their memories. The development of the Tadpole, or Pollywog, is one of the most interesting things in nature, unless you have heard about it too often. We don't have to go into *that* again, do we?[5]

3 Frogs are so greedy that two Frogs sometimes attempt to swallow each other. According to the Law of Swallowed Bodies, it can't be done.
4 Guppy's Frog of the Solomon Islands is larger than the Bullfrog and extremely hideous. Guppy can have him.
5 When the cerebellum is removed from a male Frog, he starts looking for a mate, in or out of the breeding season. There may be a lesson in that somewhere.

THE TOAD

Toads are Toads, whether you like it or not. In all probability they will continue to be Toads, no matter how much you wrinkle your nose and say that you hate Toads. Why not make the best of the situation? Toads, by the way, do not hate the other animals. They just hop in the other direction and the smarter they are the faster they hop. Some people will not handle a Toad for fear of getting warts. As Toads do not give you warts, these people are pretty foolish. I would pick up a Toad if I felt like it but I never seem to be in the mood. The Toad is happy and contented when he is not being stepped on or run over.[1] He sits on his heels in the garden, eating insects and thinking how grand life is.[2] All he asks is another insect and life is full of those.[3] Toads look very intelligent but you can't always go by that. They consider themselves better than Frogs because they have warts and their toes are but slightly webbed. Socially, webfeet are not good. The American or Hoppy Toad has blackish spots on his yellowish underside. Fowler's or

1 Thought for Toads: Nothing is flatter than a flattened Toad.
2 Toads who are allergic to insects present a difficult problem. Let's skip it.
3 Toadologists figure that Toads are worth $19.44 apiece to a gardener because of the insects they destroy. But try selling some to the neighbors for ten cents a dozen.

Cuppy's Toad is almost the same as the Hoppy Toad but his nether surface has no spots at all. If you upset enough Toads, looking for spots or no spots, you will finally have a great deal of data on this particular point. The next step will be up to you.[4] The Toad is poikilothermal. That is, the heat of his body varies with the temperature of his surroundings. I can sympathize because I'm the same way myself. He cannot endure the cold of winter, so he digs himself into the ground and sleeps until spring. Sometimes a number of hibernating Toads will huddle together in an effort to keep warm. As they are all poikilothermal, it doesn't help much. The Toad wakes up full of pep and hops to the nearest pond for his annual tub. He sings in his bath and a thousand Toads can make quite a racket. If you cannot stand it, you can always move.[5] Anyhow, the Toad doesn't care what you think of his voice. He is singing to somebody else. When he runs out of breath he is likely to hear a soft answering chirp in a high soprano. And that, my dears, is what makes the world go round.

4 Toads always return to the same spot to sleep. No imagination.
5 There are no Toads in Madagascar.

The Salamander

Salamanders are tailed Amphibia.[1] So naturally they have tails.[2] The main thing about Salamanders is that they cannot stand the heat. If they get too warm their skin dries out and they are goners because they breathe partly through their skin and it has to be moist. So Salamanders stay in cool, damp places and never go out in the sun if they can help it. Early Man was much interested in Salamanders,[3] but he could not write articles about them. As soon as writing was invented, everybody rushed into print with the statement that Salamanders live in the fire and are incombustible. The ancients used to notice Salamanders running out of bonfires built over their holes and drew the conclusion that they lived in the fire and were just

1 You mustn't call them Lizards. Lizards are Reptilia, see?
2 But for the Amphibia we should have no Reptilia, and that would be too awful.
3 More so than Modern Man, I'm afraid.

going around the corner for a minute and would be right back.[4] The Salamander could not make such a mistake about a fellow creature, since his brain is primitive and only equipped for ordinary common sense. To be as wrong as that you have to have a cerebral cortex and other refinements peculiar to the higher vertebrates. The Spotted or Black and Yellow or Fire Salamander of the Old World was the species first studied, with the results I have mentioned.[5] Herpetologists today point out that these Salamanders are unusual in that the pairing takes place on land. What's so strange about that? Most of our American Salamanders pair in the water because that is considered correct over here. Romance seems to be the Salamander's only interest. He does not realize that life is full of other wonderful things, such as — er — other things, and he doesn't care how silly it looks. Walbridge has learned a great deal about Salamanders by snipping off bits of them here and there to see what will happen. The Salamanders don't like it.[6] In spite of this new light on the subject, one still meets people who believe that Salamanders live in the fire, and they all want to argue. That's why I seldom go out any more.

4 But nobody ever saw a Salamander running into the fire.
5 In the Middle Ages it was held that asbestos is Salamander's wool. It is not!
6 A decapitated Salamander cannot make quick decisions.

The Newt

The Newt is just one of those things. You don't have to know
about him but you probably will sooner or later. You may as
well read this and get it over with. The Newt is a small kind of
Salamander and I'm afraid he is weak in the head. In fact, he's
the fool of the family.[1] After a few months as a greenish infant,
or larva, in his native pond, the Common or Spotted Newt
decides that there must be more to life than a lot of water. So
he crawls out on land to see the world and hides under a log
for a couple of years.[2] He is now an adolescent Newt, or Eft,
orange-red instead of greenish, with a row of black-bordered
vermilion spots along each side, and very pretty he is, too. Efts
vary in length from one and three-eighths inches to three and
three-eighths inches, including the tail. If you subtract the tail
there is not much left of the Eft. Efts are educational, for children find them in the woods and take them home to ask what
they are. "I don't know," says Father, and Junior stores up this

1 A correspondent inquires, "What is the advantage of being intelligent?"
Well —
2 Some Common Newts do not come out on land at all — the brighter ones,
probably.

answer until the time comes to pass it on to the next generation. Finally the Eft decides that living on land is no good whatever. Nothing ever happens on land, and when he comes out from under the log there's always Junior. He can't take it. So he goes back to the water as an adult Newt the next April[3] and learns that the mating season for adult Newts and Newtesses is in full swing. He catches on immediately and never leaves the water again. He likes it there.[4] We have many species and subspecies of Newts. Twitty's Newt of California is a large one. The average adult male Twitty's Newt is six and eleven-sixteenths inches long.[5] Newts used to cost ten cents apiece but they have gone up. If you have a Newt in your Newtery, try to face the fact that he is only a Newt. Don't go around telling little anecdotes tending to prove that your Newt is smarter than other people's Newts. What if he did climb out of his Newtery and you found him under the ice box? Who cares?

3 He has turned to greenish as a permanent color — too bad.
4 John Q. Newt is never heard griping, "Oh, to be an Eft again!"
5 One adult male Twitty's Newt is on record as 7 $\frac{3}{32}$ inches long. What a Newt!

Octopuses
and Those Things

❖ ❖ ❖

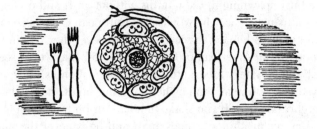

THE OYSTER

The Oyster is so small when he is born that you cannot see him without a microscope. Something generally swallows him by mistake before he becomes visible.[1] Only one Oyster in a million is lucky enough to grow up and be stewed. The infant Oyster swims around for a few days by means of his microscopic cilia, or eyelashes. If he had any sense he would continue to do this for the rest of his days, but he has other ideas. He starts to develop a shell, sinks to the bottom and fastens his left valve[2] to some solid object with a little bag of cement which he carries with him for the purpose. He thinks he is fixed for life. Ah, youth! The Oyster has many enemies such as the Starfish, the Whelk, the Oyster Drill, and the Slipper Limpet.[3] He also has friends who move him about from one Oyster bed to another so that he will be fat and healthy and a credit to the Pelecypoda, or bivalved mollusks. When he is four or five years they tell him that he ought to be more of a mixer and see more people and pretty soon he is on his way to the Grand Central Oyster Bar.[4] Oysters are good all the year round but you never heard an Oyster say that. They

1 He was hardly worth seeing anyway.
2 I would call it his left shell but let's be scientific.
3 The Piddock is perfectly harmless.
4 Some hold that Oysters have no nerves. I say an Oyster on the half-shell is a nervous Oyster.

are busy spawning in the months without an R and prefer to be undisturbed, as who wouldn't?[5] European Oysters change from male to female, or vice versa, whenever they feel in the mood. To an American or Canadian Oyster that would seem just silly. Oysters hibernate in the colder months. A frozen Oyster feels fine as soon as he thaws out unless he has been roughly handled. If you shake him hard or hit him when he is frozen, his machinery comes apart and he is never the same Oyster again. Pearls are found in the Pearl Oyster of tropical seas, if you don't mind diving among the Sharks.[6] A safer way is to hunt for pearls in taxicabs, where they are sometimes lost or thrown away by bored society leaders. There's millions in it, but you need some financial backing before you take it up as a regular business, because you might not find an abandoned pearl necklace the first few days. And the meter keeps right on going.

5 Don't believe all you hear about Oysters. The Emperor Vitellius ate twelve dozen Oysters for supper one night and nothing happened.
6 Pliny the Elder says pearls are formed by drops of dew falling into the Oyster when he is yawning. Can't something be done about that man?

THE CLAM

Clams lead quiet, uneventful lives for the most part. Buried in the mud and sand between the tide marks, or farther out in the water, they seldom get around much or hear any important news. Clams don't know what it's all about. They have no heads, so they do not bother with that sort of thing. By burrowing rapidly downward, however, Clams often outwit animals with heads. It is surprising what one can do without if one has to.[1] Clams are only invertebrates. They are among the humbler members of the mollusk tribe, yet they would be quite content with their lot if the higher forms of life would let them alone for a minute. Though they lack college educations, Clams are far from stupid in many ways. They are strongly opposed to the recent trend toward Clam culture. It looks fine on paper but they feel that there is a catch in it somewhere. For one thing, exponents of Clam culture are a little too fond of Clam chowder.[2] There is always a chance that a Hard Clam will

1 Clams are very conservative. They voted against having heads in the Ordovician Period and have stuck to it ever since. They never adopt a new idea until it has proved its worth.
2 Clams do not care whether chowder contains milk or tomatoes or what. That's the last thing they worry about.

wake up some morning under a sign reading "Certified Clams Fresh Daily." His children frequently land themselves jobs as Little Necks and Cherry Stones with Chili sauce. The Indians of the Atlantic coast made their best wampum, or money, from the purple margin of the Hard Clam shell. Quantity production of imitation wampum by the white settlers gave the Indians more leisure to think about life.[3] The Soft or Steamed Clam has only himself to blame. When crammers approach, he squirts up a jet of water to show he is home. If Soft Clams would realize how foolish this is, I'm sure they would stop it.[4] There are many other kinds of Clams, all of great interest when one is hungry.[5] Mr. and Mrs. Clam are blah and untemperamental when out of their native element, but we do not really know how they behave in a wild state. If you ask one of them what goes on down there in the mud, he shuts up like a Clam. So what does the Clam teach us that will help us solve our own little problems? Not much, probably.[6]

3 I don't understand economics, but I can see that something is wrong here.
4 The so-called "neck" of the Clam consists of his inhalant and exhalant siphons, used in feeding and what not. If he had a neck, it would be at the other end, where his head might have been. Or would it?
5 Cockles are small bivalves allied to the Hard Clam. The English eat them instead of peanuts.
6 The Giant or Man-eating Clam is found in Malaysia

THE SNAIL

What is the main thing about a Snail? That's right, the Snail is slow. He believes in taking it easy, and he is so slow at it that one gets all tired out just watching him. Following a Snail around for any length of time makes me a total wreck. I don't know why I do it. When a Snail wants to go anywhere, he travels on the underside of his physique, twitching himself along by wavelike contractions of the muscles. This is not a satisfactory means of locomotion, if you've ever tried it, and carrying your house on your back at the same time would hardly improve matters. A thought like that would never occur to a Snail.[1] The average Snail moves at the rate of two inches per minute, or ten feet per hour, and he has to stop and rest every few minutes. He might overdo. He could finish the hundred-yard dash in thirty hours flat if he kept going that long. Snails need more pep, and they won't get it by living on lettuce. Snailologists seem to be doing nothing at all about this. They're not so swift themselves.[2] A Snail never hurries to an appointment. He is sure that his date will be a day or two

1 Snails do not concentrate.
2 In a notable series of experiments, Feldkamp proved that the Snail's sense of taste is best developed in the region of the mouth. Ho, hum!

late, anyhow, so what's the use? On the way there, he generally finds some nice little Snail looking for someone who promised to be on the corner last Friday. That is why so many Snail couples consist of two other Snails. This doesn't bother Snails much. Even if they have never met before, they act as though they had known each other for years. Both of them lay eggs after a while and the children are hatched in July and August. This fifty-fifty arrangement seems odd to an outsider, but there it is.[3] The Garden Snail and the Edible Snail are happiest in wettish places, as they require a great deal of moisture to keep fit.[4] They are afraid they will dry up and blow away if they aren't careful, so they are always hoping for a stretch of damp, muggy weather. When we are tempted to complain about the humidity, let's try to remember that it's good for the Snails.

3 Marine Snails are different. For instance, a Periwinkle is either a mamma Periwinkle or a papa Periwinkle and no nonsense. Whelks and Limpets, too.
4 Land Snails used to live in the ocean, but moved ashore. Since nobody had told them otherwise, they expected the land to be as wet as the water. We all make mistakes.

THE OCTOPUS

The Octopus is much misunderstood. He is always judged by his appearance, which leaves him nowhere. In making up their minds about an animal, most people place too much emphasis upon mere external beauty, entirely neglecting such matters as character and inner worth. I have a slight tendency to do this myself but I'm trying to get over it.[1] Octopuses are not nearly as awful as they are supposed to be. They are shy by nature and prefer to avoid larger forms of life. Shyness can be overdone but in an Octopus it is a very lovable trait. The Octopus hides among rocks in the sea, waving his arms and attaching them by their suction cups to any object within reach. He is after a square meal of Crabs and other seafood, not you at all.[2] If he catches you by mistake, it isn't his fault, is it? He has you, however, and he doesn't let go, because that is the way Octopuses are.[3] Never attempt to pry his arm loose from your torso. He has seven other arms. Just squeeze his neck as hard

1 I'll let you know how I make out.
2 There are too many people around who think an Octopus is after them. They can be very tiresome.
3 Octopuses do not develop their minds. They get by and that's all they care.

as you can and he'll stop. If this doesn't work, try to think of something else quick.[4] Octopuses are cephalopods, or head-footed mollusks. The head and foot are combined, so that neither is quite what it should be. This would not do for us, as we use our feet a lot and they have to be good. The mouth is near the middle of the foot, which is divided into eight arms, or tentacles, and what looks like the head of the Octopus is the rest of his body. That's why his neck is up where it is. As if that weren't enough, they have blue blood.[5] The Common Octopus is smallish, measuring only a few feet from tip to tip. The Giant Octopus is much larger and I strongly advise you to keep out of his den. The Movie Octopus is terrific. Sometimes a male Octopus goes through a special routine for a lady Octopus he admires. He changes from brown to yellow, red, purple, violet, and blue, and flexes his biceps, four or five at a time. After watching this for an hour or so, she turns pink and everybody's happy.[6] Octopuses often become all wrapped up in each other, tangling their sixteen arms in a ferocious embrace. When Octopuses tangle it is really something.

4 You'll find his neck a few inches above his eyes. I almost forgot to tell you.
5 This is caused by the presence of hemocyanin instead of hemoglobin, as in most people.
6 The hen Octopus hangs her eggs on a rock at the bottom of the ocean and squirts water on them until they hatch. I'm not criticizing. I'm just telling you.

THE SQUID

The Squid is an important member of the Cephalopoda,[1] or head-footed mollusks. Let's have that understood from the start. The Squid and the Octopus are not at all the same animal, although one of my best friends insists that they are. I know all kinds of people. Both the Squid and the Octopus swim backwards and squirt ink, but that's not the whole story. The Squid has a streamlined, cylindrical body and ten arms, while the Octopus has only eight arms and his figure is simply a mess. Two of the Squid's arms are for grabbing things at a distance and the rest are for grabbing things closer. Why we did not develop in this way is surprising. Long, long ago the Squid possessed an external skeleton, or shell, which he changed to an internal skeleton in order to improve his swimming.[2] This is a difficult trick. It has to be done gradually or you run into trouble. Then he reduced his new skeleton until now it is only a slender, horny vestige of no use to anyone. The Cuttlefish, a cousin of the Squid, has a similar remnant con-

1 Pronounced as you like, or you might try getting used to Ceph´-a-lop´-o-da, favored by Webster — saves you from doing it differently every time.
2 Olympic swimmers never have external skeletons.

taining carbonate of lime, so at least it is good for Canaries.[3] Like all the other Cephalopoda, Squids employ jet propulsion for greater speed. They have done this for millions of years and they are still using water for power, imagine! They've never even heard of the Machine Age.[4] When he is after a fish the Squid drives himself backwards at about 10 M.P.H. by squirting water straight ahead from a gadget in his neck. Since he cannot keep his eye on Point A, where the fish was when he saw it, he soon arrives at Point B and catches another fish altogether. Or it could be the same fish, who swam over from Point A for no reason.[5] That is the technique of fishing backwards. The Giant Squid is gigantic. The Common Squid is less than a foot long. Common Squids feel wonderful in the spring.[6] They get together on nights when the moon is full and whiz backwards, facing the bright light and pumping water through their necks like mad. They often forget to stop the machinery as they approach the shore and find themselves aground on the beaches. Moral: You can't be too careful.

3 Cuttle bone just happened to work out that way. Cuttlefish never heard of canaries.

4 Walbridge states: "The Squid has missed having what might be called a brain only by the narrowest of margins." A miss is as good as a mile, Walbridge.

5 As a rule fish in their native element do not remain stationary for any length of time, especially when something is chasing them.

6 Walbridge reports that the captive Squids studied by him were monogamous. Of course, there were only two in the tank.

THE SEA SERPENT

Sea Serpents are large marine animals of most unusual habits and appearance. They are observed only in warm weather, generally in August or September, when they occasionally rise to the surface long enough to relieve the monotony by a change of climate and scene. Then they return to their homes at the bottom of the ocean and stay there until they feel low in their minds again. Sea Serpents do not come up as often as they formerly did because of what people say about them. No sooner are they seen in one place or another than somebody points out that there is no such thing. Some people think they are awfully smart. As no specimen has ever been captured, Sea Serpents have not been studied as carefully as most other animals and comparatively few persons know anything definite about them. That is where I come in. Sea Serpents are greenish on top and yellowish underneath. They have long, slender necks and tails, but the size and shape of the body are problematical, since most of it is always under water. Estimates of the total length vary from slightly less than fifteen feet to about twenty-three miles and a half. Eyewitness descriptions of the

Sea Serpent differ so much that many thinkers have given up the whole thing as too difficult. The conflicting accounts, of course, merely prove that there are several kinds of Sea Serpents. There must be. The Norwegian Sea Serpent has a horselike head the color of seaweed, a long green mane resembling seaweed, and numerous humps or bunches along his back also resembling seaweed.[1] The ones with red manes and flaming eyes are a rare subspecies. Those without manes may be females.[2] The New England Sea Serpent looks exactly like an old tree trunk bobbing about on the waves, with the roots sticking up like horns.[3] The Miscellaneous Sea Serpent is an exception to all rules. The Loch Ness Monster was of this

1 The pursuit and capture of a large piece of floating seaweed by Captain Frederic Smith of the ship *Pekin* on December 28, 1848, proves nothing whatever. That could happen to anybody.
2 The Sea Serpent noticed circa 1555 by Olaus Magnus, Archbishop of Upsala, was a very large Norwegian kind. See cut.
3 As witnessed by the Reverend Cheever Felch of the U. S. S. *Independence* in Gloucester Harbor on August 26, 1819.

type.[4] So was the object sighted by five naval officers on a fishing trip near Halifax in 1833. Boy, was that a party![5] In my opinion Sea Serpents have survived from prehistoric times, when the world was young and foolish. Most professors say it is impossible that any of those creatures should still exist. They may be mistaken. I constantly meet people who are surprised that I still exist.[6] One thing about Sea Serpents appears to be certain. Either you see them or you don't. Those who do have always impressed me as jolly good fellows and convivial companions with interesting points of view and a ready flow of conversation. Those who don't are often pretty drab. Many people go through life without ever seeing even a little one. I've never seen but two of them, myself.[7]

4 As was the one encountered by the Reverend John McCrae of Glenelg, Invernesshire, and the Reverend David Twopenny of Stockbury, Kent, in the Sound of Sleat, when sailing from Glenelg to Loch Hourn, August, 1872.
5 Compare the peculiar species described, somewhat differently, by every man aboard the Minnie, bound for Liverpool with a cargo of rum, 1872.
6 The Sea Serpent is not, strictly speaking, a snake, or reptile. As he resembles the Giant Squid in certain details, I am placing him tentatively among the Mollusca, if you were wondering.
7 Nothing is known about the love life of the Sea Serpent. It must be horrible.

How to Swat a Fly

Being as sound in mind and body as I am ever likely to be, I have decided to release my notes on Fly-swatting made from time to time during many years of active service at my Long Island beach cottage, Chez Cuppy. (It's the same old place I used to call Tobacco Road, but I think the new name sort of lends a tone — and, besides, it's a change.) In the belief that Flyswatting is here to stay for awhile, DDT and other squirts to the contrary notwithstanding, I am passing on the torch in Ten Easy Lessons, as follows:

1. Get set. Be sure you're not going to fall off your chair backwards in the act of swatting. Here as elsewhere, style is everything.

2. Still, don't take too much time with the preliminaries. The Fly won't wait there forever. He has other things to do with his time.

3. Try to ascertain in some unobtrusive way whether the object you're after is actually a Fly or a nail head, such as often occurs in the woodwork of country homes. Don't go poking at the thing to see which it is. When in doubt, swat.

Little situations like this are bound to occur in every swatter's routine. For instance, there is a small black spot on the ceiling of my bedroom that has embarrassed me dozens of times, it looks so exactly like a Fly of some large and vicious species. If I have crept up on it once — Oh, well! Stalking an imperfection in the paint and swinging one's heart out at a nail head are not things one likes to remember, but perhaps they have their place in the give and take of daily living. We can't be heroes to ourselves every instant.

4. In any case, never flirt your swatter back and forth past a Fly before swatting, expecting to get him your next time around. When you finally make up your mind to hit him, he will not be there. The Fly who hesitates is lost. He knows this and acts accordingly.

5. Take aim quickly but carefully. A complete miss is not good for the morale, either yours or the Fly's.

6. If possible, fix him with the first swat. Failure to do so may be serious. For one thing, you didn't get him. That alone is bad. Secondly, conditions will never be quite the same again, since you are now dealing with an alert and disillusioned Fly. He is never going to trust you as he did before. He will avoid you in future.

That was one of the many faults of my dear Aunt Etta's swatting. She never hit her Fly the first time and she seldom came anywhere near him on repeated attempts, partly because she employed that worst of all swatting techniques, the folded newspaper, or slow motion, method. She would lunge at the Fly again and yet again with her antiquated weapon in a free-for-all that left her exhausted and the Fly in the best of health and spirits. A folded newspaper is only about 17 per cent efficient in anybody's hands, and Aunt Etta's form was nothing to boast of. Her batting average must have been something incredible. I'm glad to state that she often thought she had won. Her eyesight wasn't so good, either.

I assure you that Aunt Etta was one of the kindest persons

I have ever known, though not so soft about Flies as my Uncle Toby, who did so much in his day to encourage the spread of typhoid fever and other diseases. There was certainly no sadistic urge in her swatting activities. She never engaged a Fly in hand-to-hand combat until after she and we children had staged a ceremonious Fly-drive with kitchen aprons and dish towels, then a second and often a third to chase the last one out the open screen door. It was only the Fly or Flies who failed to respect these rites that she tackled, and it always amazed me that there would be any such. If we thought Aunt Etta had one of her headaches, or felt a nap coming on, or couldn't stand such a racket — in which case she would tell us so in no uncertain terms — we disappeared. We vanished utterly, with the usual gift of cookies. But Flies are not brought up that way, apparently. They cannot take a hint.

The family would want me to add that Aunt Etta's house was no more Fly-ridden than any other home of the period. In fact, it was less so than most, as it was thoroughly screened. Which reminds me that she never did, to my knowledge, solve the riddle of how they got in. She was always saying there wasn't a crack where they could squeeze through. All right, then, how did the Mouse get in?

7. Don't mind a little incidental breakage around the house. Aunt Etta was much too careful of her bric-a-brac. She wouldn't strike within yards of her whatnot when a Fly took sanctuary there. For the cause I would smash anything in Chez Cuppy to smithereens, except possibly my shaving mirror. I'm not having seven years of bad luck for any Fly.

8. Cultivate patience. It is a beautiful thing in itself, and when you are after a Fly who will not light, you will need it. Eventually that Fly will light, and ten to one it will be in some dark, inaccessible corner, down behind the stove.

The Fly who absolutely refuses to settle is a problem for advanced swatters, and not an easy one. Talk about a watched pot! Do not stalk such a Fly too openly, but try to act as though you were interested in something else altogether. This involves looking wall-eyed at the Fly while gazing fixedly in the other direction, but it can be done, with practice. It is my opinion that a Fly will not settle while you are looking straight at him with a swatter in your fist. At any rate, he won't while you are following him around the room, making passes at him. Believe me, he knows what you are up to.

I would go so far as to say that a Fly knows the exact moment when you start looking for a swatter, if you should be caught without one. Edge yourself ever so casually in the general direction of a swatter, and notice what happens. Other persons who may be present will simply wonder why you are hitching your chair along in that insane fashion or tiptoeing across the room with one groping hand outstretched and a haunted look in your eyes. They won't have the faintest notion of what goes on, but the Fly will. He has already figured out his first five moves and several of yours.

This does not necessarily prove that the Fly is more intelligent than you are. If such things could be measured — and they will be, some day — I have little doubt that you, gentle swatter, would be found to have a higher I.Q. than the average Fly. You may be slow on the uptake, while the Fly is unbelievably fast. His sheer brilliance in planning and executing maneuvers of every sort on the ground and in the air amounts to genius, and you have all you can do to keep from falling over your feet. You cannot make quick decisions, or, if you do, you are generally dead wrong, as everybody at the office knows but yourself. The Fly's decisions are mostly right. They have to be.

Yet on the whole, taking it by and large, and allowing for individual exceptions, you are smarter than the Fly. You know more than he does about more things. Above all, you possess the power of abstract reasoning, a faculty which distinguishes mankind from the merely brute creation, such as Flies. You can listen to the radio, look at television, and go to the movies. You can read mystery stories and try to guess who done it. Keep your chin up and always remember that if you are not the Fly's superior in every single respect one might mention, you are at least his equal, mentally. Since you are fighting on practically even terms, then, when you are after a Fly who will not light you must seek for a flaw in his intellectual equipment if you hope to gain the initiative, and I can help you there. The key is his imperfect memory. You can remember as far back as yesterday. The Fly cannot. He forgets. The particular Fly of whom we were speaking will be out of his dark corner in a few brief moments, and you can begin the whole show all over again.

9. Check up on yourself occasionally. Ask yourself, "Am I a better swatter than I was last year?" The correct answer is No.

10. Don't be discouraged at a few failures. I don't always get them myself, but I give them pause. It makes 'em think.

INSECTS
FOR EVERYBODY

❖ ❖ ❖

THE ANT

Ants are very industrious but they don't seem to get anywhere. They have been doing exactly the same things for millions and millions of years and they never learn any new tricks. I'd say they are in a rut. Entomologists regard Ants as the most successful of the insects, if you would call that a compliment.[1] Since Ants belong to the social hymenoptera, they exist only for the community or Ant hill as a whole and do not develop their individualities. They are interesting enough as a group, if you like that sort of thing, but when you get one of them alone he is apt to be rather a bore.[2] An Ant community contains one or more queens and a few males with wings and many workers without wings. The males are only waiting around for the nuptial flight, after which they die off and the

1 Entomologists are people who want Ants around. If there are no Ants around, they will go where Ants are.
2 The small-headed types are the worst, but at least you know where you are.

queens start laying eggs like mad. The Ants you find in the sugar bowl are workers. That's their idea of work. Ants operate by instinct instead of intelligence. Intelligence is the capacity to know what we are doing and instinct is just instinct. The results are about the same.[3] Some species of Ants are extremely clever, for Ants, but we can do everything they can do and we're not always getting stepped on, either.[4] Harvester Ants store up seeds for a rainy day.[5] Ant authorities now agree that these Ants do not actually plant the grain. I could have told them that. Harvester Ants just gather the seeds and grind them into flour and mix it up into little cakes and set them out in the sun to bake. Leaf-cutting or Parasol Ants live entirely upon certain fungi which they cultivate in their Ant hills. Entomologists are not quite sure how they do this. I hope they find out.[6] There are many other Ant problems, but the main one is how to get rid of the darn things.

3 But we do it on purpose.
4 An Ant on a hot stove-lid runs faster than an Ant on a cold one. Who wouldn't?
5 The one King Solomon wrote about was *Messor barbatus*, a harvesting species, or so they say.
6 Parasol Ants carry umbrellas made of leaves, except when it rains.

THE BEE

As we learn from history and folklore, Bees have been with us from the earliest times. The Ancient Egyptians considered it good luck to meet a swarm of Bees on the road. What they considered bad luck I couldn't say.[1] Honey Bees are by far the best kind of Bees, as they believe in helping others. They make honey for us by gathering nectar from the flowers and changing the sucrose into dextrose and levulose, which is more than some people can do.[2] They also cross-pollinate the flowers by carrying pollen from blossom to blossom. We could do this ourselves but it would take an awful lot of time and we are not built for it.[3] The workers, or neuter Bees, never accompany the queen and the males on the mating flight. They stay

1 The first person to study a Bee carefully was very much surprised. He didn't know it was loaded.
2 The Ancient Chinese had a saying, "Bees make honey and men eat it." Maybe I don't get it.
3 Worker Bees have pollen baskets, or corbiculas, on their hind legs. Other Bees have just ordinary legs.

home and spend the day making more honey. They expect to retire on their savings, but they die of exhaustion in about six weeks. The males, or drones, do nothing but buzz around all summer and eat up the honey. In the fall they are killed by the neuters to conserve the food supply. Drones think their fun will go on forever. If you tried to teach them that life is not like that, it wouldn't do any good. Sometimes Bees get to feeling that everything would be all right if only they were somewhere else. So they swarm out of the old hive and hang to the limb of a tree and a man with a veil on his hat comes and brushes them into a box and takes them away and everybody's happy.[4] Until quite recently people who owned Bees made a point of telling them about all the important or unusual events in the family, in order to keep them contented. This custom was known as Telling the Bees. It is fast dying out because there is too much to tell nowadays. Anyhow, Bees are totally deaf. Honey Bees sting only once. Bumble Bees sting whenever they feel good and like it.[5] Sometimes a Bumble Bee will get into a flower and can't get out. That's too bad.

4 City Bees like to swarm on policemen. Why that is, your guess is as good as mine.
5 I understand the Bee employs twenty-two different muscles in the act of stinging. So what?

THE CRICKET

Crickets chirp a lot. That just about covers the subject of Crickets except for a few minor details. The House Cricket, or Cricket on the Hearth, starts chirping at dusk and chirps all night. That makes it nice for the people who live there, for Crickets sound so cheerful and cozy. Some people can't get to sleep unless they hear Crickets chirping. They will bring Crickets in from the country and turn them loose on the hearth. Sometimes I think I don't understand life at all.[1] Field Crickets chirp in the daytime too. They often move into the house when the weather is cool.[2] Field Crickets eat woollen and linen goods, but only when they are hungry. Some people begrudge them even a small piece out of a suit of clothes. Have Crickets no rights? The Snowy Tree Cricket, or Temperature Cricket, is the most useful kind. According to Edwin

1 Lettuce leaves, apple cores, moist bread and bone meal scattered around the floor at bedtime will make them chirp louder and longer.
2 Crickets would rather be warm than almost anything else. I'm the same way myself.

Way Teale, the Snowy Cricket's rate of chirping varies with the weather so exactly that you can find the temperature in Fahrenheit degrees by dividing the number of chirps per minute by four and adding forty.[3] If you have a thermometer but no Cricket, multiplying the degrees of Fahrenheit by four and subtracting one hundred and sixty gives you the number of times the Snowy Tree Cricket would have chirped per minute if you had had one. The thermometer offers you more for your money.[4] It does the work of both and you don't have to climb a tree to get at it. Only the male Cricket chirps. He does it by rubbing his tegmina, or front wings, together, thus throwing the tympana of the tegmina into rapid vibration.[5] Scientists now tell us that the Cricket is not chirping a love song to his mate, as most of us have always believed. They say he chirps just to be chirping and that he is not a bit romantic. The fact remains that when you find one Cricket under a piece of old newspaper you always find two. But I'm not going to argue about it. I don't care enough.

3 A few Crickets chirp faster or slower than they really should. Can Professor Teale help it if you try the wrong Cricket?
4 The Snowy Tree Cricket cannot tell you what day of the week it is. He doesn't know.
5 Crickets have their ears on their front legs. Nothing surprises me any more.

THE MOSQUITO

Mosquitoes teach us that there's always something.[1] But why not look on the bright side? Only the females bite and they don't do it for meanness, they just want a square meal. Mosquitoes are only trying to get along. As the proboscis of the male is weak, he lives on nectar and plant juices and never bites, no matter how hungry he is. He probably would if he could. In some sexes both species are perfectly harmless. The next time you hear a Mosquito humming around your ear, remember that certain Mosquitoes in Tierra del Fuego are strict vegetarians.[2] Male Mosquitoes react to the humming of female Mosquitoes. By amplifying the hum of a female Mosquito, entomologists have succeeded in drawing hundreds and even thousands of male Mosquitoes to the scene of the experiment, where they are shocked to death. This leaves the female Mosquitoes without any mates and the birth rate

1 Mosquitoes are mentioned by Herodotus, if that helps any.
2 I am often asked why Mosquitoes hum loudest when close to one's ear. I don't know.

immediately falls.[3] Mosquitoes pass their youth in the water where the eggs were laid. The larvae or Wigglers wiggle around and hang head downwards from the film formed by the surface tension of the water. This sounds like a poor thing to hang from, but it seems to work.[4] Wigglers are awfully cute. Many people can watch them wiggle for hours. Others find it a trifle tedious after a while. The final aquatic stage lasts only a day or two because the young Mosquitoes are in a hurry to squeeze through a screen door and guess what. The Salt Marsh or Beach Mosquito is extremely abundant in some places.[5] The Domestic or Rain Barrel Mosquito gets you in other places.[6] Domestic Mosquitoes often spend the winter in cellars and attics, emerging in the spring to lay their eggs. But not if I see them first. Still and all, statistics show that only one Mosquito in a million ever bites anybody, so let's be more cheerful about it.

3 Different species of Mosquitoes have different love hums, so you must be sure to imitate the right one. It all depends on the kind of Mosquitoes you want to attract.

4 Surface tension is what makes a drop of water round. I never heard of it until this minute, but that proves nothing.

5. *Aëdes excrucians* inhabits British Columbia and Alaska.

6 *Culex damnosus* is found throughout North America.

THE GNAT

Gnats get in your hair. They get in your eyes and your ears and make themselves quite at home. They always feel perfectly welcome. You can't insult a Gnat by brushing him off. He comes right back with more Gnats. The average Gnat is only one-tenth of an inch long. You can imagine the size of his hat. There's a little speck in his head that may be a brain. Gnatologists can't decide whether it is or not, unless there have been new developments as we go to press.[1] I don't worry about it myself because a brain you can't find without the aid of a microscope wouldn't be much of a brain anyhow. As a Gnat's thoughts are extremely small, a regular brain would be a waste of gray matter.[2] When they are not annoying people, Gnats keep flying around because they live but a short time and they're afraid they might miss something. Male Gnats are tricky. A lot of them dance in the air together, and it is surpris-

1 The fact that such a problem should arise is pretty significant.
2 The Gnat has an exoskeleton, or external skeleton, formed of a layer of $C_{30}H_{50}N_4O_{10}$. There would hardly be room for it inside.

ing how many lady Gnats happen to be going that way while out for a constitutional. Naturally, they stop for a moment to see what it's all about. That is why we always have plenty of Gnats. Some species of Gnats are harmless. They follow you around but they do not bite. They just go for the ride. Others nip you at sight. It's the only way they have of attracting attention. Biting Gnats include the Buffalo Gnat, the Turkey Gnat and the Yellow Gnat.[3] The smallest and worst is the Punkie. Punkies live in beautiful lake and mountain regions and they bite something fierce, although they are only one twenty-fifth of an inch in length. They swarm all over you, looking for weak spots in your clothing, and act accordingly. The Indians call these insects No-see-ums.[4] The Indians have several other names for Punkies, none of them very flattering. One could keep out of places where there are Punkies, but one never thinks of those things until later.

3 Little is known of the Splay-footed Gnat, at least by me.
4 Most Gnat writers explain the meaning of this term at considerable length. I haven't time now.

THE BUTTERFLY

Butterflies are the most beautiful of all the insects, and maybe they don't know it! They flit from flower to flower and every move is a picture. They are good for nothing except to look at. Maybe that is enough.[1] The only interests Butterflies have are food and romance. They do not eat very much as they consider it a waste of time. The mother Butterfly lays her eggs on plants and flies away and pays not the slightest attention to the Baby Butterflies, or Caterpillars. You can hardly blame her.[2] Some Butterflies travel in groups at the rate of fifteen miles per hour, going just anywhere they happen to go. Monarch or Milkweed Butterflies, however, go south for the winter. Lepidopterists, or Butterfly professors, are always asking, "How do they know which way is south?" They just do, that's all.[3] Lepidopterists also wonder what can possibly induce Monarchs to undertake so long and arduous a trip. Well, why *would* anyone

1 Fact is, we could use more of such insects.
2 Pliny the Elder says Caterpillars come from the dew on radish leaves. Yes they do!
3 The professors will deny this. Sounds too easy.

go south for the winter? Science tells us that the brilliant coloring of certain Butterflies is a warning to insectivorous animals that they are not good to eat and should be left strictly alone. But sometimes a Butterfly meets an animal that has never heard of the theory of conspicuous coloration. Then he is out of luck.[4] The Leaf Butterfly of the East Indies is a nervous type. He folds his wings above his body, bringing the brownish side into view, hides his head between them, and clings to a twig all day long. In this position he resembles a dead or dying leaf and believes himself to be safe from his enemies. Unfortunately, he also resembles a Butterfly trying to look like a leaf.[5] There may be something in it, since the Leaf Butterflies all do it, but I wonder what they get out of life. The young of the Cabbage White Butterfly simply love cabbage. That must be why our cabbage back home never seemed to come to a head. Something was wrong with our lettuce, too.

[4] Birds and Bats are unable to follow involved lines of reasoning when hungry.
[5] And what do they do about things that eat leaves?

114

OPTIONAL
INSECTS

❖   ❖   ❖

THE BEETLE

Speaking of Beetles, it is simply amazing what goes on under stones and old boards and loose bark.[1] Coleopterists, or persons who frequent such places, have found 250,000 species of Beetles and there are probably a million more waiting around to be discovered. You and I may never know the exact number of existing Beetle species and just how each one differs from all the others in physique, let alone what they do for a living and the opinions held by the individual members on things in general. I can face it if you can. We have all these species because Beetles do not know what they want. They lack any real goal in life, but they keep tinkering with themselves in the hope that something worth while may develop. They don't seem to grasp the fact that in any event they would still be Beetles.[2] That's where they made their mistake in the first place. Most Beetles possess hard elytra, or non-flying forewings, to prevent squashing and protect their posterior flying wings from injury while at rest. There is a feeling among Bee-

1 Forty per cent of all insects are Beetles, according to one count. Some say forty-one per cent.
2 Law of nature: Once a Beetle always a Beetle.

tles that you're only as good as your posterior wings, and this strikes me as a sound idea. That's about all I can hand them. Beetles never make the front page. The Granary Weevil, however, has been on the radio.[3] The giant Hercules Beetle ruined his looks by growing long curved horns on his head and chest, so that he resembles part of a Lobster going along in front of a Beetle. If he had anything in mind he forgot what it was, and now he is stuck with that face.[4] Beetles always make sure that the supply of Beetles equals the demand. The Ticking Beetle calls his mate by knocking his head against the woodwork. Well, that's one way.[5] The male Bark Beetle has as many as sixty wives at a time. One of these fellows is said to have lived in a certain pine tree for thirty years. It may have been the same tree but I don't believe it was the same Beetle.

3 He was terrible.
4 The female Hercules Beetle never grew horns. You can imagine what she thinks.
5 Tapping on the furniture with the thumbnail will often evoke answering ticks, but it strikes me as a rather pointless proceeding.

THE FIREFLY

Fireflies are nocturnal in their habits. They sleep most of the day and only come out at night. All animals who do this will bear watching. Naturally, certain persons are constantly checking on the movements of Fireflies, noting where they go after dark and what happens when they get there. These persons are called Firefly observers, and there are several species.[1] Professor Jones used to roll home at three A.M. when he went out to observe Fireflies. He said they were at their best after midnight.[2] Dr. Halstead tells me, however, that Fireflies turn off their lights and go to bed at eleven p.m. As Dr. Halstead invariably retires at that hour with a black silk handkerchief over his eyes and plugs in his ears, I hardly know what to think. There has been a good deal of loose talk about Fireflies because they light up their abdomens before they start out of an evening, a proceeding that strikes some people as perfectly outrageous, to put it mildly. I don't believe half I hear about the female Glowworm, a wingless member of the

1 They are nocturnal too, but that's different.
2 And so was old Jonesy, decidedly.

family. At dusk she climbs a stalk of grass and switches her lantern in every direction, but how do we know that she is trying to lure a male Glowworm to her side? Maybe she's just waiting for a streetcar. The male Glowworm has wings but is only feebly luminous.[3] Among our commoner Fireflies, both boys and girls have luminous arrangements and it is difficult to say which side does the more flashing. It would seem to be about fifty-fifty.[4] The Cucujo, a large tropical Firefly, is so brilliant that it is possible to read a newspaper in the light cast by a single specimen held in the hand and moved along the print. But two are better.[5] The light produced by Fireflies contains practically no heat rays and therefore it does not hurt them.[6] Firefly professors have tried for many years to learn the secret of this cold light so as to make it in quantities, but I wonder if they would be any happier, really, if they could light up their abdomens. Why not let well enough alone?

3 Well, that's the way it is in some families.
4 When Firefly observers join in the fun with pocket flashlights, the insects go away after a minute or two. Fireflies are easily bored.
5 The Cucujo displays two green headlights when at rest and one red light aft when flying. Makes you think, eh?
6 Some of our leading scientists have written rather fully on this subject. I don't understand it either.

THE LADYBUG

Ladybugs are pretty little things with fresh, natural coloring
and pleasing ways. They haven't a great deal of sense but we
love them just the same. Most Ladybugs dress in polka dots,
especially black dots on red or yellow material. Others use red
or yellow on black as a striking novelty. A few Ladybugs try
splotchy prints and appliqué effects in contrasting shades, but
they only look out of step.[1] Polka dots are always good.[2] As
Ladybugs are roundish and plumpish, some people think they
should cultivate stripes. If they wore stripes they would be
Potato Bugs. Besides, Ladybugs have no waistline whatever
and there is no use pretending that they have.[3] The Ladybug
is one of our best insects.[4] She destroys Aphids and Scales,
those nasty little creatures that damage plants. But for her
we would have no orange juice for breakfast because of the
Cottony Cushion Scale, and the Aphids would increase so
enormously that they would kill every plant in a few years.
Then all life on this planet would cease, and how would you

1 The Perplexing Ladybug is hard to describe. It would take volumes.
2 The Two-spotted Ladybug and the Fifteen-spotted Ladybug both go to
extremes, but you can't argue with them.
3 The Potato Bug is plump, stripes or no stripes. Either you are, or you
aren't.
4 Good insects are those who do what we want them to do. The others are
bad, or noxious.

like *that*?[5] Since she does so much for us and is so cute, the Ladybug has been a favorite insect through the ages. We teach our children to be kind to her and never harm her in any way, so you know what happens whenever they see her. The male Ladybug is very shy and retiring. He is fed up with hearing people exclaim, "Oh, isn't she the darlingest thing!" In some species he omits the polka dots. Late in autumn Convergent Ladybugs of both sexes go to the tops of mountains to get away from it all and sleep through the winter. They huddle under the snow in tightly packed masses containing millions of individuals.[6] Then Ladybug dealers dig them out and put them in cold storage until they are wanted by somebody who has Aphids. A Ladybug's work is never done. Some people believe that a Ladybug, when observed by a young woman, flies straight toward a place where there is a likely fellow, thus helping girls to find husbands. She doesn't do this. She has her own troubles.

5 Ladybugs, or Ladybirds, are not bugs, but Beetles. You are a bug only if you belong to the order Hemiptera, formerly the suborder Heteroptera. Is that clear now?
6 Ladybugs are not classed as social insects. If that isn't social, what would you call it?

THE FLEA

Fleas are remarkable jumpers. For this reason they are often compared to the Kangaroo and the Chamois, though the resemblance is not very striking.[1] A Flea one-twelfth of an inch long, weighing an eighty-thousandth of an ounce, can broad jump thirteen inches and high jump seven and three-quarters inches.[2] Flea admirers are always wondering what would happen if a Flea were six feet tall and strong in proportion. Well, his brain would be so much larger that he would be able to wonder how far a man could jump if he were only one-twelfth of an inch long. If men were as small as Fleas, it would be pretty discouraging. So maybe things are better the way they are. Fleas jump partly because they have no wings and partly because they are Fleas. All six of their legs are attached to the front part of the body near the neck, completely ruining their shape. I worry sometimes but not about that. Most of our common Fleas belong to the family *Pulicidae*, and what a family![3] The Human Flea is supposed to bite

1 The Chamois is a little animal used for polishing windows.
2 More Flea statistics of this kind should be made available to the public. What good are they if they're filed away somewhere, gathering dust?
3 The Yokuts think the Pleiades in the constellation Taurus are five girls and a Flea. True or false?

only humans, but has been found on Weasels, Hogs, and Polecats. Dog Fleas come from the people upstairs. An animal who harbors Fleas is called a host or hostess. Some Fleas are extremely choosy about their hosts and hostesses. There is a Flea who will bite only the Long-tailed Field Mouse. He would rather starve than bite a Short-tailed Field Mouse. He is unusually large and can jump only one inch. He doesn't want to jump. He just wants to be on a Long-tailed Field Mouse. The female Chigoe or Jigger Flea[4] of warm countries burrows into one's skin and stays there to develop her eggs. Some insects have a nerve.[5] Educated Fleas can dance, play the drum, juggle, and draw wheeled vehicles, but they are poor in arithmetic. Both sexes bite. I'm afraid I have neglected the emotional life of the Flea. Frankly, I don't know how a couple of Fleas feel about each other. Ask somebody else, can't you?[6]

4 Or Bicho.
5 Our own Chigger is a Mite, not a Flea. No relation.
6 Aristotle occasionally wrote on the Flea — and not from hearsay.

THE FLY

I hate Flies and I don't care who knows it. They may not like me much either, as those things generally work both ways. House Flies are full of germs and bad manners. They come to the table and act something awful. They have a positive gift for the wrong gesture at all times and places. They spend their lives annoying others, but they probably think they're a big help. Well, they're kidding themselves.[1] House Flies walk upside down on the ceiling to show how smart they are. They can do this because they have pulvilli, or sticky pads, on their feet. As they are practically glued to the ceiling, they couldn't fall off if they tried, so what is so bright about it?[2] Flies have only two wings. Instead of hind wings they have two threadlike projections which look something like balancing poles and are therefore called halteres, or balancers. A Fly loses his equilib-

[1] Certain philosophers hold that Flies are as good as we are. I have my blue Mondays, but not that blue.
[2] The force of gravity doesn't work very much on Flies because they are so small. They're not worth bothering with.

rium and cannot fly if you remove his halteres. If you snip off any other portion of his physique, he also acts funny. The one decent thing about the House Fly is that he does not bite. That is because he can't.[3] Nor does the Lesser House Fly, often taken for an adolescent House Fly.[4] The Fly that bit you was a Stable Fly, of either sex — as occasionally happens, one is as mean as the other.[5] The female Horse Fly attacks horses, cattle and some people. The male drinks plant juices and flies around checking up on conditions. The Thick-headed Fly is fairly abundant. I have no doubt that he always will be. The social behavior of the male Fly is rather at random. Some male insects mate and die. The male Fly mates and mates.[6] A young Fly never knows who his father was. I could go on with his family tree, but I might say something I'd regret.

3 If the House Fly could bite, it would be just too much! I for one would be totally disorganized every summer.
4 The Lesser House Fly arrives earlier than the House Fly to get us used to the idea.
5 The Stable Fly in a house is sometimes called the Biting House Fly, but that's just a quibble.
6 Although he is slightly smaller than she is, the male House Fly's eyes are larger than hers. He misses little or nothing.

Swan-upping, Indeed!

I was a fool to give Swan-upping a second thought. I won't say I should have ignored it. You can't ignore a thing that is called Swan-upping. The moment I heard of it, I should simply have said, "Swan-upping, eh?" or "Fancy that!" and gone about my business, instead of spending an afternoon in the Public Library reading about Swans.

Swan-upping sounds like a custom that should have been quietly dropped around the time, say, of Ethelred the Unready. But it has not been dropped — that's the whole point. Indeed, it flourishes, quite as it did on July 16th, 1308, when Edward II issued a commission of oyer and terminer about some Swans belonging to John de Fresingfeld, who kept his birds on the Waveney, at Mendham, Suffolk.

The Thames, of course, is *the* place for Swan-upping now, and July or August is the month, depending upon the pleasure of the Vintners' Company, the Dyers' Company, and the King of England, who divide the Swans on the river among themselves and annually up, or take up, the young ones and mark them on the bill with a penknife to show who owns which.

In the course of centuries England's Swan laws have attained such perfection that almost everybody has been seriously inconvenienced, from the King down. For instance, whenever Swan laws were broken, especially in regard to taxes (or Swannage), the King was supposed to seize the said Swan or Swans appertaining thereunto, and sometimes he didn't want any more Swans. Nothing, by the way, can get on one's nerves like too many Swans.

Or sometimes the King wanted all the Swans he could possibly obtain, and the Queen hated the very sight of them. The King would prepare to seize some Swans. The Queen would be firm. I shouldn't wonder if there was Swan trouble between Edward II and Isabella the Fair. She had him murdered, you know.

Then there's the law that any person found carrying a Swanhook, the same being neither a Swanherd in good standing nor accompanied by two certified Swanherds, or Swannerds (or Swanners, or Swanmasters), of known probity, should cough up thirteen shillings fourpence, three shillings fourpence going to the informer and the rest to the King. This looked like a fine bit of legislation until it developed that you can't collect from such people. They haven't got it. That's why they're out stealing Swans.

The strange thing is that anybody should try to carry a Swanhook around without attracting a lot of attention, let alone get by totally unobserved. A Swanhook is a rather cumbersome and conspicuous affair, generally attached to a long pole, by means of which it is possible to up, or capture, a Swan by the neck. It is not an object to be easily concealed about the clothing. Either you are carrying a Swanhook or you aren't.

We seldom hear of these miscreants nowadays. They seem to have lost interest. Doubtless they grew tired of telling inquirers, while making for the nearest Swannery, that they were only trying to get a cat out of a tree. The provision that they must be accompanied by two Swanherds probably discouraged them, too. It is a well-known fact that when you need a couple of Swanherds, you can't find even one.

Time was when simply mobs of festive Londoners would follow the Swan-upping barges along the Thames, either afoot or in gaily decorated boats. There would be cold collations and dancing on the grass while the uppers of the Dyers and the Vintners and the King, dressed respectively in blue, blue-and-white, and red jerseys, merrily upped the young Swans, or clear-bills, at Kingston, Stains, Maidenhead, and Henley. Of late the turnout has been sparser, and it has usually rained.

Nor are Swan-marks what once they were. The Vintners have got down to two nicks on the bill and the Dyers to one. The King's uppers don't even bother to nick the King's Swans any more. They just go along for the ride.

Things were very different among the old Dorset Stour crowd. The Abbot of Beaulieu, or Old Bewley, as everybody called him, marked his birds with only four short lines, but the Prior of Christchurch always insisted upon a small square in sinister chief, a black spot on the sinister edge of the middle of the bill, and a small circle in the middle of the lower half of the bill, with a line proceeding from it, sloping to dexter. A bit showy, perhaps.

Whatever I may think of Swan-upping as a sport, if such it be, I have no intention of trying to stop it. I know only too well what happened to the gentleman who once replaced

with silk cord and tassels the long leather thongs attached to the purses used at the ceremony of the Maundy money at Westminster Abbey. He was told to take the cords and tassels off and put the leather thongs back where they belonged. At the same time, I understand, a certain person gave him what could only be interpreted as a look. And quite right, too.

Birds Who Can't
Even Fly

◇ ◇ ◇

THE OSTRICH

The Ostrich is our largest living bird. A full-grown male Ostrich is eight feet tall and weighs three hundred pounds stripped. He is really too big for a bird and it must make him feel rather foolish.[1] Because of his size, the ancients regarded the Ostrich as part quadruped, even though he has only two feet. It is possible to think of a biped as half a quadruped if you have that sort of mind, but the proposition will not hold up in the long run. In order to settle the matter, Aristotle took a close look at an Ostrich and announced, "It differs from a quadruped in being feathered." Just came to him in a flash, I suppose. The story that the Ostrich sticks his head in the sand when pursued, in the belief that this action renders him invisible, has brought undeserved ridicule upon the bird. It was started by Pliny the Elder, runner-up to Aristotle as an authority.[2] Can the Ostrich help it if some people are not very

1 Flightless birds like the Ostrich are called Ratitae, as their flat breast-bone reminds birdologists of a raft, the Latin word for which is *ratis*. Oh, well!
2 Although the old tale teaches us nothing about the Ostrich, it does shed light on the mental processes of Pliny the Elder. Shows what he would have done if he had been an Ostrich.

bright?[3] The popular notion that Ostriches subsist largely upon a diet of horseshoes is quite erroneous. They swallow sand, nails, and glass to promote the digestion of their food, which includes watches, doorknobs, and pieces of old machinery. Horseshoes are merely an occasional luxury.[4] The Ostrich's egg is about the size of a coconut. It contains as much egg as eighteen ordinary hens' eggs and is somewhat gamy. One of them makes a meal for two to six Hottentots, depending upon the size of the Hottentots. You boil it for fifty minutes and call in the Hottentots.[5] The Male Ostrich in search of a wife seeks to interest the prospect by displaying his feathers, dancing before her, fanning her with his wings, and uttering strange popping noises. As often as not she pays no attention whatever, but the male Ostrich seems to make out all right. He is frequently seen wandering around the desert with four or five females who lay their eggs in his nest and help him hatch out the young. This has given rise to certain rumors which I prefer not to discuss. I never repeat that kind of gossip unless I practically saw it myself.

3 Pliny the Elder perished in 79 A.D. when he refused to flee from the great eruption of Mt. Vesuvius, insisting that everything would be all right. It wasn't.
4 Horseshoes lack certain essential vitamns. They are harmful when swallowed to excess.
5 An Ostrich egg is a natural for the emergency shelf. Just the thing for friends who drop in unexpectedly.

THE EMU

The Emu is a three-letter bird found in Australia. Don't drop everything, now, and go rushing off to Australia to see him. You'll be sorry if you do because what you see when you see an Emu isn't so much. The Emu is about five feet tall to the top of his head when he holds his neck up straight. He has stringy grayish-brown feathers and no pretty plumes on his wings and tail and big flat feet with only three toes on each one. He looks like a second-hand Ostrich.[1] The female Emu is somewhat larger than the male, who sits quietly on the eggs while she speaks her mind in a peculiar booming voice amplified by an air sac connected with the windpipe. This gadget enables her to vocalize continuously except when she is asleep or unconscious from a swift kick in the beak.[2] Half of the time Mr. Emu doesn't know what she is booming about. She doesn't say. To an outsider it sounds like "Blah, blah, blah," with an occasional "I told you so."[3] After the children are hatched, Mr. Emu leads them out for their morning meals of fruit, roots,

1 The humerus of the Emu is surprisingly short.
2 Emus believe in monogomy, or one Emu at a time. At least that's the theory.
3 Few Emu couples can truthfully state that they have never had a cross word.

grass, and the small stones required by the Ratites or flightless birds for digestive purposes. He watches them carefully, admonishing them from time to time in a low buzzing tone. This means, "Eat your pebbles, you little Ratites!" Emus have been domesticated with considerable success, but there is a drawback to having them around. You must not run away when the Emu approaches or he will chase you and behave rather roughly when he catches you, as he undoubtedly will.[4] He always senses it when anyone is afraid of him and acts accordingly, so you must pretend to be quite indifferent.[5] The correct procedure is to stand perfectly still when an Emu comes at you with his wings outspread and blood in his eye. He may possibly change his mind or drop dead before it happens.[6] If you feel that you simply cannot face the Emu, of course you can try to escape. In making the choice, a good deal depends on where you would rather be kicked. Anyway, getting kicked by an Emu is no worse than lots of other things. Life isn't a bed of roses, you know.

4 His kick is less severe than that of the Ostrich, which easily breaks a man's leg. The Emu's kick seldom breaks more than the fibula, the smaller bone of the leg, leaving the tibia in first-class condition.
5 He senses that, too.
6 See Dr. Feldkamp's vivid account of this bird in his *Wanderings in Eastern Australia*. Written up a tree, apparently.

THE KIWI

The Kiwi is a flightless bird found only in New Zealand. I am often asked why Kiwis are not found in other countries. As they cannot fly, how would they get there? Dr. Feldkamp, the Kiwi expert, states that the ancestors of the Kiwis lost the power of flight in the Miocene Age, many millions of years ago, because they were too lazy to use their wings.[1] Or maybe the early Kiwis just didn't get the idea that birds are supposed to fly. Maybe nobody told them. The Kiwi's wings are now so small and weak that he doesn't know he has any.[2] His tail is rudimentary, he lacks a wishbone, his feathers are more like hair, and his nostrils are at the very end of his extremely long beak instead of where they belong.[3] It is no use trying to improve him, for there would always be something you forgot to fix. Kiwis live mostly upon Earthworms. When they tap on

1 In a recent conversation to me, Dr. Feldkamp admits — for the first time, I believe — that he was not an eyewitness to events in the Miocene.
2 The scientific name of this bird is the Apteryx, meaning that he has no wings whatsoever. He has so.
3 Kiwis constantly make a sniffling or snuffling noise through their nostrils. Whatever causes this, it can be most annoying.

the ground with their strong feet, the Earthworms come to the surface and are swallowed. Dr. Feldkamp says the Earthworms believe it is raining when they hear the taps and come up to get wet.[4] But perhaps they only want to see what is going on, as who wouldn't? The female Kiwi is about as large as a large Hen. She is famous for laying the biggest egg in the world in proportion to her size. It measures three by five inches and weighs a pound, or one-fourth as much as she does. I suppose I shouldn't worry about it.[5] The male Kiwi is smaller and louder than the female. Sometimes he will whistle shrilly at a female Kiwi. If she answers with a softer call, his social schedule is all arranged for the season.[6] Pretty soon she lays one of those eggs and chirps, "Well, that's over, thank goodness!" Then she gives him a nasty look and he has to sit on the egg until it is hatched, while she takes a good rest and builds up her constitution. During the period of incubation in the dark underground nest he utters no sound. He's said too much already.

4 I forgot to ask him how he found this out. Remind me to wire him.
5 The old story that the Kiwi's egg is larger than the Kiwi herself is untrue.
6 Kiwis are so called because they are always saying "Kiwi-kiwi." That could mean anything.

THE MOA

The Moa of New Zealand was the largest bird that ever lived.[1]
His fossil remains show that he was ten or twelve feet tall and
weighed five or six hundred pounds. I believe that some day,
if we dig deep enough, we will find a Moa who was at least fifteen or sixteen feet tall and weighed eight or nine hundred
pounds, and then we will really have something.[2] I just know
he is down there. No other scientist can make this statement.
The Moas attained their great size thousands and thousands
of years ago when there were no people or other dangerous
mammals in New Zealand and whole forests of giant ferns to
eat. So they stuffed themselves with ferns all day long and
grew bigger and bigger, for ferns contain plenty of nourish-
ment if you eat enough of them. As they had no wings, naturally, the Moas could not fly.[3] They just wandered around in
pairs. And why not? Then all of a sudden they became extinct

1 Some say the Aepyornis of Madagascar was a bit larger. I doubt it.
2 Aepyornis, indeed!
3 They had no wishbone, either, and no pygostyle, or plowshare bone, at the
end of their tail. That turned out to be pretty serious.

and nobody knows how it happened. Dr. Feldkamp thinks they perished in the severe volcanic eruptions of the Pliocene. The weakness of this view is that volcanoes do not, as a rule, pursue any one species of animal to the exclusion of all other kinds. Why would they kill off the Moas and leave the Kiwis safe and sound? Answer me that.[4] In my opinion the personal habits of the Moas had much to do with their eventual fate. All they did was eat, sleep, and have little Moas, and towards the last there was even a sharp decline in the birth rate. They couldn't be bothered.[5] At this point it was up to the Moa to take more exercise, eat less, and lead a different sort of life altogether. Then he would have been a healthier and a happier bird, full of pep and in a far better frame of mind to survive. The Moa did not do any of these things because, unfortunately, he was not as intelligent as I am.[6] Besides, a bird who can't fly is merely making himself ridiculous and he may have realized it. So maybe it's all for the best. If the Moas were still alive, they would be here in the U.S.A. by this time, running around every which way looking for ferns. They would be all over the place and goodness knows traffic is bad enough as it is.

4 Those Moas the Maoris said they exterminated about five hundred years ago were only little, no-account Moas the size of a Turkey. Not our species at all.

5 You might say they were bored to extinction.

6 I attempt to prove this in my more advanced course on the Moa.

BIRDS WHO CAN'T SING AND KNOW IT

❖   ❖   ❖

THE PELICAN

The Pelican is strictly a fishing bird. He goes fishing every day. What is more, he catches something. He does not come home and say that the wind was wrong and they weren't running, just like the last time he went fishing. Of course, the Pelican is built for it. He has a large elastic pouch attached to his lower jaw, which enables him to scoop up fish under water and carry them to the surface to swallow them. As this is a most unsightly object, few of us would want it on our face, but it does the work and that is all the Pelican cares about.[1] The Brown Pelican of our Atlantic coast dives right into the water after the fish, without any fooling around. The White Pelican of the Pacific coast chases the fish into shallow water and then scoops him up, if he is still there.[2] While the Pelican is draining the water from his pouch and preparing to swallow, the Laughing Gull often grabs the fish and flies away, laughing like anything.

1 In some parts of the world the Pelican's pouch is dried, embroidered in various colors, and used for holding snuff. It's the ideal Christmas gift.
2 Cornering a fish in any large body of water, such as the ocean, is a tricky business. Fish have ideas, too.

The Pelican has no sense of humor. He would not see the joke if you explained it to him over and over again, with diagrams. Yet some people believe that fish are good for the brain.[3] Pelicans think only of fish. Nothing you can think about fish is very deep. Pelicans possess a strong social sense. They fly together, fish together, live side by side on the ground, and steal nesting material and fish from one another whenever they get a chance.[4] White Pelicans fly north in the spring to breed on islands in fresh-water lakes. The Brown Pelican is more of a seagoing type. He breeds where he is.[5] The male Pelican walks slowly round the lady Pelican, uttering low groans and yawning. He is not demonstrative, but he is steady and reliable and that's something. Baby Pelicans are simply awful. The female Pelican feeds them on predigested fish served in her pouch. When they become too greedy and noisy and generally unbearable, she closes her bill and hits them on the head with it, so that baby Pelicans are always staggering about in a dazed condition, squalling for more fish and getting whammed on the head again. As the force of such blows is hard to judge, little accidents occur from time to time. That's a risk you have to take. Moral: It's a great life, if you like fish.

3 The Blue-faced Booby lives entirely on fish. Need I say more?
4 Some Pelicans nest in trees but they shouldn't. Birds in trees should be smaller than Pelicans — a whole lot smaller.
5 The Brown Pelicans of the east coast of Florida mate in October or November. They can't wait till April.

THE DUCK

Ducks are very interesting, if you like that sort of thing. Of course they are not Nightingales or Birds of Paradise. They're only Ducks. Duckology is simple enough once you get the hang of it. After the first few lessons you should be able to tell a Duck from a Goose.[1] If you can't, just step up to somebody and ask, "Is that a Duck or a Goose?" That's what I do. The male Mallard is easy to identify, as he has a green head and neck, a white collar, and a rich chestnut chest. A trifle gaudy, I sometimes think. The well-dressed Duck is never conspicuous. Like most male Ducks, he is much fancier than the female, who sticks to subdued browns and grays and always looks right for any occasion.[2] Male Mallards shed all their flight feathers at once during a special postnuptial molt every summer and cannot fly until they grow out again. So what do they do? They lose their brilliant colors and turn sort of drab and brownish, like

1 Hint for beginners: The Duck is more Ducklike.
2 The male Gadwall is one of the duller Ducks. He is brighter than his wife, but not much.

the females, hoping to escape the notice of their enemies while in this helpless condition.[3] Well, they wouldn't be helpless if they shed their quills gradually, like other birds, and they could do it in the regular fall molt, without all this nonsense of grounding themselves and changing color and skulking among the reeds. One molt a year is enough for anybody, goodness knows. A little sound thinking along these lines might do the male Mallard no harm.[4] According to some Duckologists, Mallards have only one mate. I heard different. Male wild Ducks experience no real home life, as they take no part in building the nest, hatching the eggs or rearing the young. They don't know what they're missing.[5] Puddle Ducks just wander around the barnyard and swim in dirty puddles. They do not believe in germs. Commercial Ducks have modern ideas. The Long Island Duckling is a big success at the age of three months, with applesauce. The Canvasback feeds on wild celery in the Chesapeake Bay region, thus improving his flavor and raising his price in the market. Pretty smart for a Duck.[6]

3 The female may be distinguished by her loud, clear and repeated "Quack! Quack!"
4 Unfortunately — but you see the difficulty here.
5 The male Gadwall flies hither and thither, crying "Whee-you! Whee-you!" This is said to mean "Nice weather we're having."
6 The Bufflehead — well, you get the idea.

THE GOOSE

There are forty different kinds of Geese in the world. It seems as if there were more. The main problem about Geese is whether they are foolish as they are supposed to be.[1] Dr. Feldkamp says the average Goose has a mental age of three weeks.[2] On the other hand, Pliny the Elder states that Geese are extremely sagacious. But would he know? Pliny based his opinion on the old tale that a flock of sacred Geese saved Rome from the Gauls in 390 B.C. by cackling and gabbling in the night, thus arousing the citizens to their danger. Ever afterwards the Romans held Geese in the highest esteem but the Gauls were so sore that they went back home and invented *pâté de foie gras*. I don't think those Geese had the faintest idea that the Gauls were approaching. Geese wouldn't know a Gaul if they saw one. They simply felt like making a racket at that unearthly hour, so they did.[3] The fact remains that a good

1 Favorite remark of Early Woman to Early Man: "Oh, don't be a silly Goose!" His reply is unknown.
2 If I had time I would tell you more about Dr. F.
3 No proof exists that a flock of Geese saved Rome, either on purpose or accidentally, but to Pliny the Elder it was the gospel truth. That man would believe anything.

deal of history has been made by Geese. Sometimes a Goose will take a fancy to you and follow you around whenever you go, stopping when you stop and starting when you start and cackling every foot of the way about things that do not matter in the least. You can't get a word in edgewise. Some people naturally attract Geese and there is nothing much to be done about it. You just have to grin and bear it. Or leave town. A Goose always accompanied the philosopher Lacydes, head of the Academy at Athens, having singled him out when a mere Gosling as a congenial companion. They can tell. Personally, I don't expect any sense from a Goose, so I am never disillusioned. Their feathers are nice and soft and they lay Goose eggs and the Goslings are wonderful. What more can you ask? You have to take Geese as you find them. That's the way they are meant to be. Common Domestic Geese are monogamous. They look it.[4] Wild Geese migrate in flocks, or gaggles, flying in V-formation and honking as loud as they can.[5] When they fly north in March they are hailed wherever they pass as harbingers of spring. Everybody stops work and rushes outdoors, shouting happily, "Geese! Geese! Spring is here!" I generally go right on with what I am doing. I know when spring is here.

4 It is said that Geese choose their mates on Saint Valentine's Day. I always forget to check on it — too busy with my own problems.
5 The mating call of the White-fronted or Laughing Goose is "Ha! Ha! Ha! Ha!" What's so funny?

THE SWAN

Swans have been studied by so many great minds through the ages that we now have quite an accumulation of nonsense about them. The Greeks said Zeus made love to Leda in the form of a Swan. In my opinion that wasn't Zeus, that was only an old Swan.[1] Nor do Swans sing a Swan song just before they die, as stated by Plato and Aristotle, the wisest men of their time.[2] They simply heard the rumor somewhere and rushed it into print, as usual. Some people do not bother to check their facts — it's beneath them.[3] Swans cannot sing and they do not try, thus differing from several birds I could mention. They haven't the proper vocal muscles and they know it. The Whooping Swan of Europe[4] and the Whistling and Trumpeter Swans of North America make loud whooping noises that can be heard for a couple of miles, but they don't call it singing.[5]

1 They also reported that Leda then laid two eggs, out of one of which popped Helen of Troy, out of the other Castor and Pollux. Nothing in it.
2 I often wonder what the others were like.
3 Plato, in the person of Socrates, describes the song of the dying Swan as one of rejoicing. Aristotle says it is mournful. No comment.
4 This is the kind Zeus was supposed to be at that time.
5. The whistling Swan does not whistle.

They can do this because their extra long windpipes are coiled, or looped.[6] The more familiar Mute, or Tame, Swan is not mute. He has no loops, so he cannot whoop, but he hisses fiercely when angry, as he generally is, with or without reason.[7] In the mating season Mute Swans entwine their necks and utter low sounds, like everybody else. They mate for life, especially when their wings are clipped so that they cannot fly away.[8] The Pen, or female, is a little smaller than the Cob, or male Mute Swan and her neck is more slender and graceful. She is truly an enchanting sight as she floats on the lake with her neck full of curves and her pure white wings partly raised to catch the breeze, watching for someone to throw her a bun. On land she is not quite so perfect, as her legs are too short for easy locomotion and you can't help noticing that she is web-footed. She ought to stay in the water.[9] By the way, the Swan dive is not practiced in Swan circles. Swans cannot dive. The Swan is hard to write about because so much that we know of him isn't so. Even Shakespeare went slightly haywire whenever he got on the subject. It does something to you.

6 The Trumpeter Swan has one more loop than the Whistling Swan. He is now very rare.

7 Bird lovers formerly carried raised umbrellas to avoid attack by enraged Swans. They finally learned that Swans have no respect for tradition.

8 Swans live to be forty or fifty years old, not a hundred, as we were all taught in school. Sometimes they feel like a hundred.

9 Bewick's Swan has loops.

MORE ABOUT WOMBATS

It has been brought to my attention, none too tactfully, that a book with the word "Wombat" in the title should contain more about Wombats than seems to be the case with *How to Attract the Wombat* up to the late point I have now reached, and I thank God I have reached it. I suppose the fellow meant more words by actual count, irrespective of the force and cogency of the words I had already written. "More about Wombats" is the way it was put to me, and that's all I can tell you.

Since I do not speak this person's language, I can only guess at his meanings and motives. All I really know about him is that a heavy glass bowl of Goldfish fell on his head when he was two years old (accidentally, he says), that what came out of him at the moment of impact you wouldn't believe, that some really valuable fish perished in the excitement, and that he survived to become a power in the literary world of New York, one whose least suggestion it is folly to disregard and ruin to oppose. H'm!

When he butted in the other day, as I was showing the outline of my book to somebody else, I had the distinct impression that he had never heard of a Wombat before. "Wombat!" he exclaimed. "Did you say *Wombat?*" I was looking straight into his face, if you could call it a face, and I could see him struggling inwardly for some frame of reference, as he would phrase it. I replied rather coolly, "Why yes, I said Wombat."

It took him exactly one minute to recover his poise, grab my synopsis, fix all four eyes on the last line, and make his considered judgment: "More about Wombats." If I had let him, he would have gone on to tell me that it would contribute to the esthetic effect of the whole, sort of knit it up, as it were, if I had more on the Wombat right there. He's all for those *da capo* effects in his own writings, always pounding away at his opening stuff as much as the traffic will bear, then harking back to the damn thing at the end, when all you want on this earth is to forget it. I understand he used to recommend that bit of technique — and a fine one it is, in its place — in his English One class at the University. It's very funny how he happened to leave there, too. I wish I had time to tell you.

Mind you, when this happened I was celebrating the completion of my manuscript, a state of affairs roughly comparable to release from a long jail rap into the sunlight and freedom, joyful communion with the birds and the flowers, and access to other phenomena too numerous to mention. I mean there is a considerable difference to the author between a book that is finished and a book that is not. So what did I do? I could have taken that one over the eight and called for another on top of that. But you know me. One dirty look from however low a source and I go in for soul-searching — the sober, or most painful, kind.

To spare you the details, I found that I do have a slight tendency to write books purporting to teach how to do thus and so, and that I am too likely to stray from the main point, or omit it altogether, leaving the reader in what has been called, for some reason I have never quite understood, the lurch. Obviously, this is wrong. It may very well affect certain types with a sense of unfulfillment, an uneasy suspicion that they have been had. In a way it is only fair that I should explain the Wombat a little more fully, as long as I brought the subject up in the first place.

Since I did not tell everything I know in my earlier remarks, perhaps a paragraph or two on the Wombat as a pet would not come amiss. The burrowing habits of which I spoke offer the Wombat owner an interesting first-hand study of a true tunneller, whether the animal is digging into the underpinning of your residence or honeycombing the yard with subterranean passages in all directions. As Wombats seldom succeed in bringing down a large, solidly constructed house, you may as well dismiss your fears on that score and take a chance. Naturally, some people are unnerved at the thought that the Wombat is out there doing his best. Just forget it.

When the Wombat is excavating a tunnel, note that he often lies on his side, digging at the earth with his claws and his hard nose, an organ which is beautifully adapted to the purpose. You don't see that every day. Once he has started a tunnel, it is practically impossible to get him out again, for Mother Nature impels him to proceed until he has gone a hundred feet or so along under the sod and constructed at the end of the passage a nesting chamber for his comfort and repose. Even if you catch him at the mouth of the hole and attempt to extract him with a lasso or a shepherd's crook, you can't. He just braces himself against the earth with his powerful hands and feet and remains there indefinitely, a real lesson in endurance and stick-to-it-iveness.

Nor can you dig him out with any degree of success. He keeps ahead of you and before you know it you are spading up the adjoining back yard like one possessed. Neighbors being what they are, you are in for a little discussion on just what you think you are doing. This is known in the courts as Wombat trouble.

If there are small children around, they are sure to find a Wombat's burrows wonderful places to explore. They will probably crawl into one of them in an effort to reach the bark-lined nesting chamber and establish a playhouse there, a marvelous prospect for them but one which should be discouraged in view of possible cave-ins and total lack of ventilation. Such an adventure cannot be good for a child, and actual harm might come of it. Simply tell them not to go near those burrows that the Wombat made and you should have no further difficulty. If that doesn't work out, I'm sure some remedy can be found, short of getting rid of the children.

Having the yard full of holes, of course, might be dangerous even to grownups who are not willing to watch where they're going. Wombat holes have proved to be something of a nuisance to horses and cattle in Australia and Tasmania, and the stories that have drifted over here about it frighten the timid. Nonsense! You can stay in the house if you have to and observe your Wombat or Wombats through the window. If you must go outside, be careful, that's all. Wombat fanciers with exceptionally brittle bones might do well to have the condition attended to. If such persons are too lazy to see a doctor, they should at least take large doses of whatever vitamins are good for such things, try to build up their resistance with a spring tonic — some calcium mixture, perhaps — and they will soon be ready to own a Wombat. The wheel chair simply yawns for persons who will not take even the most ordinary precautions. Why blame it all on the Wombat?

Wombats who are kept outside need hardly any care. In a state of nature their diet consists largely of grass and the bark and roots of young trees and shrubs. If there is anything of the kind in your yard, it would be nice for the Wombat, and you could do lots of research on his gnawing methods. If you have a favorite tree you want gnawed, it might be simpler to get a Beaver to do it. Beavers accomplish more in the same length of time and they work longer hours.

The Wombat who is kept inside the house also deserves a word in any Wombat manual such as this. Like any nocturnal creature, he sleeps most of the day in his straw-filled box, snoring contentedly and somewhat loudly, if you care for that. About all this gets you is the opportunity to say you have a pet Wombat, a simple truth which is hard to demonstrate to visitors. All they see is a patch or two of brownish fur under the straw, but some of them are willing to believe that what they are looking at is a Wombat. The straw in the Wombat's box should be changed every few days. Every few minutes would be better.

At night the Wombat wakes up and starts living. If you strongly disapprove of this routine, and I find many people do, you might hint to him that no good will come of it, that there is no sense in it, and that you do not do it yourself. Tell him to stop sleeping his brains out in the daytime and go to bed at a decent hour, and you might add that we were never intended to turn night into day. You will then have done your duty as you see it, but I doubt if the Wombat will pay much attention. I am constantly receiving similar advice myself and it appears to make no perceptible change in my schedule. Some are built that way, some aren't. It would be my guess that the Wombat has no desire to be more like other people.

If you resemble the average pet owner, you should be able to cope handily enough with the Wombat's nocturnal activities around the house. You would hardly know he is there, unless you happen to hear him tearing up the floor by way of getting on with a new nesting chamber. You'd better do something about that, too. I suggest that you have the floors of your home reinforced with a layer of concrete over the boards and perhaps a layer of asphalt on top of that. Any road construction gang will do the job at reasonable rates if you catch them during their slack season. The Wombat will go through it in time, but it will slow him up considerably.

Meanwhile, you can be thinking up other measures, the more the better. Why not revise your philosophy of life a trifle and sleep during the day, even if this does involve admitting that the Wombat was right, after all? It's no time to quibble. Should your business suffer too much from the new time scheme, should you find it impossible to carry it on while most of your clients or customers are unconscious, why not retire from the whole tiresome grind and take it easy? I understand this can be arranged upon payment of a small fee or something of the sort, and the people who have done it say it is fine. You probably need a good rest, anyway. You might travel, for one thing, leaving your house and grounds to the Wombat, lock, stock, and barrel.

I trust I have shown that a Wombat in the home makes all the difference. If you require more proof, I point to the experience of Mrs. O'Connell, of Bullallaba, New South Wales, who brought up a Wombat from the age of six months and never regretted it for one moment. This Wombat loved to be fondled in her arms and would follow her around with obvious devotion until she fed him. Although he preferred lettuce leaves, cabbage stalks and milk, he would accept scraps or anything and show his gratitude, just how I couldn't say. No trouble at all.

Charlie, as we may call him, for I think of all Wombats as Charlie, added to the gayety of the O'Connell household by rolling over and by rearing up on his hind legs and attempting to butt like a goat, a trick Mrs. O'Connell seems to have found more amusing than otherwise. I fancy her as a solid old body who was not likely to be upset by any amount of butting by a mere Wombat. We are told nothing of any spells of rage, accompanied by rather nasty biting, a characteristic of some Wombats. He didn't even growl.

Although Charlie was completely free and had burrows in the garden, he never damaged a plant or a flower. Nor did he ever keep a soul from getting his proper sleep at night. Mrs. O'Connell loved to talk about him and there was no word to any of her cronies about any vices whatever. In short, if Charlie had a single fault, large or small, you'd never hear it from

Mrs. O'Connell. He was pure joy and delight as a pet and a pal. I, for one, believe that Mrs. O'Connell was telling the truth as she saw it, or at least part of it.

My file on famous Wombats of history is not as complete as I could wish, but I can give you an example or two. The first Wombat ever seen in England was taken there from Bass Strait by a Mr. Brown, a wandering botanist, somewhere around the beginning of the last century (probably in 1807, though I cannot be certain of this), and lived for two years in the house of Mr. Clift, of the Royal College of Surgeons. Here the Wombat's acquaintance was made by Sir Everard Home, the great anatomist and surgeon, whose paper (1808) on the animal has been used by naturalists ever since, generally in indirect quotation so that you can't tell what he actually wrote.

According to one scientist, Sir Everard found his new friend "not unintelligent," though no particulars are given. That's not quite the same as saying that the Wombat is as smart as a whip, though it does show that Sir Everard did not regard him as completely hopeless. The scientist throws in the following on his own: "In captivity it [The Wombat] is as a rule amiable, the amiability being possibly associated with stupidity." What do you make of that? I must say it's a fine way to speak of an animal who is trying to develop the better side of his nature, and succeeding.

In view of the varying opinions about the Wombat's mentality, one may conclude that some Wombats are brighter than others. Or perhaps it would be safer to say that some are dumber than others. Be that as it may, the most provocative, or do I mean disturbing, sentence I have encountered in my researches concerns the peculiar manner or mood of the Wombat's biting with his really formidable chisel-like teeth, a thing I mentioned in my shorter piece on the Wombat because it was essential to even the briefest report. It is fitting that we remind ourselves of it now, when we are about to say farewell to the Wombat.

The source of that information is Ellis Troughton's recent work, *Furred Animals of Australia*, where the author writes of Sir Everard's Wombat, perhaps in that great man's own words, or nearly so: "It good-naturedly allowed children to pull or carry it about, and if it bit them it did not appear to do so severely or in anger." It just bit them. You who hope to understand the Wombat will do well to read that sentence again. And reread it. And ponder.

I shall have to omit the bulk of my material on Dante Gabriel Rossetti's Wombat, the very thing I was leading up to. Christina tells us that when she lived at Tudor House with Gabriel, he had a Wombat, an Owl named Bobby, a Woodchuck, and a Deer. The Wombat slept in a silver épergne in the middle of the dining-table — a good-sized épergne, I should think, as Wombats often run to a length of forty inches. The Reverend Charles Lutwidge Dodgson used to call and there is a possibility that he turned the drowsy creature into the Dormouse of the Mad Tea Party, though I should think that if he wanted a model for a Dormouse he might have used a Dormouse. Christina put a Wombat into her poem, "Goblin Market," probably the same one.

Mr. Benson recalls other members of the Rossetti ménage without mentioning where they parked themselves: a Chameleon, a Salamander, a Raccoon, an Armadillo, a Zebu, and a Kangaroo. I have also heard somewhere about a white Bull and a white Peacock, who crawled under the sofa one day and died there — a sensitive bird, no doubt. It is clear that with such a family running around regardless, Rossetti was hardly the man to strain at a Wombat. Indeed, he had a second one after the first had passed on, which would indicate that he found Wombats a necessity in every well-regulated home, if you will excuse that imperfect description of Tudor House. The right adjective does not occur to me.

I had hoped to trace the influence of Wombats on Rossetti's poems and right on up to the works of our greatest living novelist (you heard me), Angela Thirkell, who is some sort of relative of his by marriage, I believe. The Wombat who slept in the silver épergne may well be responsible for Mrs. Thirkell's strange, almost morbid, interest in the Golden-crested Mippet. I had stuff like that, all very cultural and significant, but there isn't a minute to spare as we rush to press. Ask me later, will you? (Later: What I meant to say was that Mrs. Thirkell is the niece of Burne-Jones on her mother's side — no relation to Rossetti. As it is practically impossible to tell the two men apart, I feel that my theory still holds up.)

And now that we are bidding farewell to the Wombat, it strikes me as rather a good idea. Telling you more about Wombats has served to clarify my own views in some respects, so much so that I wonder what I could have been thinking of before. I ask myself, is it fair to a Wombat to try to lure him away from Australia and Tasmania, where he can dig up practically the whole of the antipodes if he chooses, and nobody cares? He does so love to play!

Would it not be downright cruel to keep him in semi-captivity in a town or city, where the opportunities for wreaking havoc and destruction upon the landscape are necessarily so limited? In a word, is it *right* to attract Wombats? There is a bright side to all this, however, for I have just called up the Bronx Zoo and they tell me you can't get one, anyway, unless you are an accredited zoölogical institution — and who is?

APPENDIX

❖　❖　❖

THE SCORPION

See the Scorpion. Will the Scorpion bite? No, if you are kind to the Scorpion and treat him as a friend, he will not bite you. He will sting you. Scorpions sting their prey, consisting of Spiders and insects, to make it behave while they eat it. Scorpions and Spiders are not insects but arachnids, with eight legs. Insects have only six legs. Won't you *try* to remember that?[1] Scorpions often sting people on the hands and feet when annoyed or disturbed. They also sting on general principles. They carry their tails curled over their backs and always sting in front of themselves. When you are hanging around a Scorpion, stay near his southern end. You'll enjoy it more.[2] The poison of the Scorpion's sting is seldom fatal to the larger mammals, but it hurts something fierce. One can, however, acquire partial immunity by taking the proper steps. If you let a Scorpion sting you every once in a while, the effects become less severe each time, until finally all you notice is the sensation of being stabbed with an ice pick and a slight dizzy feel-

1 Well, you needn't get sore at me. I had nothing to do with it.
2 Scorpions can be kept for observations in a glass jar with a lid on it. Don't forget the lid.

ing for several days. I have never tried this myself. What with one thing and another, I'm always putting it off.[3] The Scorpion leads a solitary life for the most part, as he has a low opinion of all other Scorpions. They hate their kind, except in May, June, July and August, when they go to the opposite extreme. In these months the Scorpion and the Scorpioness take long strolls, pincer in pincer, stand on their heads, and carry on regardless. It isn't love, really. It's more of a mad infatuation.[4] Then the Scorpioness devours her mate and that's the last of him. Seems as though this habit of hers would get around among the fellows, but those who know most about it are in no condition to make a report. Baby Scorpions remain with their mother for the first two weeks, riding on her back, frisking merrily in the grass, and growing meaner every minute. I suppose I ought to be sorry for Scorpions because they are so awful. I'll think it over.[5]

3 If you think you have Scorpions under your bedroom floor, remember that Scorpions live only five years.
4 Both partners are extremely repulsive. Fortunately, Scorpions have poor eyesight.
5 Scorpions never sting themselves to death, no matter what that nice old gentleman told you. But go ahead and believe it, if you'd rather. There's no law against it.

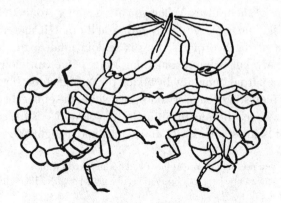

THE EARTHWORM

The Earthworm loves to work. We should encourage him in this tendency because work is so good for one's character, and somebody has to do it. The Earthworm plows the whole world with his tunnels, drains and aerates the earth, fixes the topsoil and I don't know what all, and he never asks a cent for it.[1] If you ever buy any land, be sure it has plenty of Earthworms toiling and moiling all day so that you can sit down and relax. Of course you still have to feed the Pigs and a few things like that. Don't be unfair to the Earthworm. Give him a hand now and then. After all, he is not just any worm. He is an annelid, or higher worm.[2] Earthworms hate to be called Fishworms. It gives people ideas.[3] The Earthworm is a great success at digging holes because he has solved the problem of what to do with the dirt. He eats it. The Flatworm would never think of that.[4] The Earthworm comes up at night for additional food

1 The pointed end is his head.
2 You would be surprised at the people who look down on Earthworms.
3 Wormologists believe that a fishhook does not hurt the Earthworm, as he does not yell, "Help! Murder!" They ought to know.
4 Flatworms are lower worms.

and companionship, first anchoring himself to his tunnel by his tail in order to find his way back, then stretching himself as far as he can in every direction to see what is doing around there. In this way he meets his next door neighbor, who is out for a breath of fresh air. One Earthworm alone doesn't mean much. Two Earthworms together — well, it makes all the difference. Earthworms are keenly aware of this fundamental truth. Earthworms need large families to help with the plowing, so both of the parents lay eggs. That's the spirit! An Earthworm often becomes so interested that he forgets to snap back before dawn, and guess what. The early Robin catches the late Earthworm. If the Robin is otherwise engaged until later, he pulls the Earthworm right out of his home in broad daylight, no matter how much he struggles.[5] Sometimes a Robin will stretch an Earthworm so far that the poor little Earthworm breaks in two and the Robin falls over backwards. Goody!

5 The Earthworm's reaction is an example of negative thigmotaxis, or the desire not to be eaten by a Robin,

A Note on the Type

How to Attract the Wombat has been set in a digital version of Caledonia, a type designed by William Addison Dwiggins for the Mergenthaler Linotype Company. Released in 1941, Caledonia bears the ancient name of Scotland, a reference to the type's roots in the so-called Scotch types of the nineteenth century. That the type enjoyed near-immediate acclaim upon its release is testimony to the success of its long and unusual development. Seeking to relieve the "wooden heaviness" of the Scotch types then available for machine setting, Dwiggins began by redrawing the face in the style of the types cut for Miller and Company in the early nineteenth century. Finding that Scotch "doesn't stay Scotch if you sweat the fat off it," Dwiggins went on to experiment with admixtures of the characteristics of Scotch and its most successful antecedents: Baskerville, Bodoni, and Didot. When these efforts proved to be "merely a rehash," Dwiggins turned his attention to the Bulmer type, which in combination with the structure of Scotch Roman provided the inspiration for one of the most admired book types of its time.

❖   ❖   ❖

Design, composition & digital imaging by
Carl W. Scarbrough